The
FOOLPROOF
FREEZER
COOKBOOK

The FOOLPROOF FREEZER COOKBOOK

Prepare-ahead meals, stress-free entertaining, making the most of excess fruits and vegetables, feeding the family the modern way

Ghillie James

Photography by Tara Fisher

KYLE BOOKS

Dedicated to Eva, Alice, Charlie, Leo, Florence, and Isla.
With my love x

Published in 2012 by Kyle Books
www.kylebooks.com

Distributed by National Book Network
4501 Forbes Blvd, Suite 200
Lanham, MD 20706
Phone: (800) 462-6420
Fax: (301) 429-5746
custserv@nbnbooks.com

ISBN: 978-1-906868-25-3

Editor: Catharine Robertson
Designer: Lizzie Ballantyne
Photographer: Tara Fisher
Food stylist: Debbie Miller
Props stylist: Liz Belton
Copy editor: Anne Newman
Americanizer: Jo Richardson
Index: Helen Snaith
Production: Gemma John, Nic Jones, and Sheila Smith

Library of Congress Control Number: 2012938820

Color reproduction by Alta Image
Printed and bound in China by Toppan Leefung Printing Ltd.

contents

introduction ··· 6

basics and batches ··· 16

soups, appetizers, and nibbles ··· 40

meals using frozen ingredients ··· 64

prepare-ahead main courses ··· 78

baked treats ··· 100

desserts ··· 120

babies and children ··· 150

conversion chart/oven temperatures ··· 170

index ··· 171

acknowledgments ··· 175

introduction

You only have to wander down the frozen food aisle of your local grocery store to realize that frozen foods have moved on in leaps and bounds over the past few years. Battered fish sticks and suspect chicken pies with no discernible filling have been moved aside to make way for soufflés, risottos, and charbroiled eggplant. For me this area of the supermarket was always for convenience only—frozen peas and ice cream for busy days when I had no time to cook. Now, however, I find myself ogling the canapés and tarts, scallops, and summer fruits, held back only by my purse strings.

But has our home freezing gone the same way? When there's an over-abundance of fresh fruit and vegetables in the garden that tastes at its best, are we turning berries into ice cream, or cooking and freezing a stash of fresh tomato soup for weekend lunches or an ice cube tray full of homemade Thai green curry paste for busy days and hungry children? Or what about preparing a batch of lamb tagine and a selection of frozen vodkas to pull out when friends pop over for an impromptu Friday night in front of a DVD? With so many time-stretched, nutrition-savvy, and budget-conscious families, it's the freezer, not the fridge that should be our best friend in the kitchen.

Food from the freezer needn't be dull or bland. Clear out your freezer, thaw it, then fill it with your favorite kinds of food. Whether that's a fantastic homemade curry sauce and ice cream to save on a tempting takeout, prepare-ahead canapés and desserts for a hectic Christmas, cookie dough ready to bake, or homemade pizzas ready to top when you have children to entertain on a rainy Sunday afternoon.

A freezer is *the* kitchen appliance for those who want to save money. You can make double when foods are less expensive or in season, buy produce on offer, and, most importantly, freeze your leftovers rather than throw them away. From bread crumbs to egg yolks, there are tons of leftovers that are suitable for freezing, as well as mountains of things to do with them.

The freezer should especially be a new mom's best friend. Supermarket baby food has moved on from jars of unrecognizable goop to incredibly nutritious organic jars and pouches—but sadly available at incredibly high prices. I use them myself, when we are going away for a weekend or on vacation, so that I can guarantee I have something on hand when arriving at our destination and my one-year-old daughter decides she wants her lunch NOW! However, I can't justify using them everyday, nor have I time to lovingly prepare individual meals that each take an hour to make and then spoon into jars. With my second child, I've worked out a way of making baby purées that can be quick and easy—and, I think, more nutritious as well. I've also devised some toddler food that will please the parents, too—and, no, it's not just shepherd's pie and mac and cheese!

I hope that *The Foolproof Freezer Cookbook* inspires you, gives you some handy tips, and helps you to make the most of fruit and vegetables in abundance. I also hope it makes your busy life easier—it certainly has helped mine.

Ghillie

ten reasons to freeze

1. Buy produce such as meat in bulk, and make the most of good offers and deals, then just use it as you need it.

2. Prepare and freeze local, in-season produce when it tastes at its best and costs less. You can then enjoy your favorite foods year round, without the transport costs.

3. Get ahead and prepare for entertaining in advance to prevent last-minute hard work.

4. Use half a bag of something and just freeze the rest—freezing is ideal if you are cooking for one or trying to keep fussy-eaters happy.

5. Freezing acts as a natural preservative, so you can enjoy your favorite things in their natural state, rather than bottled or jarred.

6. Get your "five a day" with ease—frozen foods often contain more vitamins and minerals than fresh, as produce can be frozen immediately, before it has time to deteriorate. Frozen peas contain up to 40 percent more vitamin C than two-day-old fresh ones, for example.

7. No need to chuck leftovers anymore—save time and money and freeze them. (See page 13 for ideas.)

8. Save time by cooking straight from the freezer instead of shopping on the way home from work.

9. Make recipes in batches when you have time and use them up in quick recipes when you don't.

10. Take the stress out of cooking for babies and toddlers with cubes and pots in the freezer that take minutes to reheat.

(F) Freezing

(D) Defrosting/thawing

(R) Reheating

(C) Cooking

(S) Serving

freezing—the rules

Always freeze produce and recipes when they are at their freshest —don't be tempted to freeze something that's past its best—it won't taste good once thawed and cooked!

Although you can refreeze food that has been properly thawed in the fridge, the quality may well be impaired due to loss of moisture in the defrosting process. Therefore it is best to refreeze previously frozen raw foods once they have been cooked.

Always make sure you wrap every item well, whether in a double layer of foil, a freezer bag, or lidded container—this will protect the food, preserve the flavor, and prevent anything from suffering from freezer burn.

If freezing liquids, always leave a bit of extra space at the top of the container, bag, or bottle to allow for expansion.

Freeze things as quickly as possible—use the "quick-freeze" shelf or function on your freezer if you have one.

Don't overcrowd the freezer because it won't work as efficiently.

Cool food as quickly as possible once cooked, and freeze it only when completely cool.

Follow recommended storage times for best quality (see page 12).

Open-freeze "wet" foods such as sausage, raspberries, or frosted cakes on a tray, uncovered, in a single layer to prevent them sticking together or ruining. Once frozen, transfer the items to a bag or container.

storing and thawing

I'm not going to start advising on which is the best freezer to buy, as to be honest I don't have a clue! However, I have thoroughly researched the latest in boxes, bags, and labels to help you freeze your food effectively, use up the minimum of space, and keep it at its optimum quality.

Take it from me, there's nothing more annoying than digging out a cake or casserole from the freezer that has either been knocked about or damaged from cold air, which causes freezer burn (dehydration patches on the food). Careful wrapping and storage will increase the freezer life of food substantially, so it really isn't a waste of money to buy some strong good-quality freezer boxes and bags, and most importantly some labels and a freezer pen.

Boxes and bags

There are lots out there, from old ice cream containers to snazzy lockable lidded boxes. Make sure the lids are tight fitting and bear in mind that if you buy a few of the same shape, they will stack well and therefore take up less space. If you are buying boxes especially for use in the freezer, it's worth checking that they are both dishwasher- and microwave-safe. I use boxes for storing cakes, meringues, tarts, and any other food items that might get damaged if bashed about a bit. I also freeze small quantities of sauces, such as applesauce and bread sauce, in plastic boxes or pots so I can thaw and then reheat them in the box in the microwave.

There are now some incredible freezer bags available. Some have zippers, which makes it easy to dip in for a handful, then quickly zip shut—they are great for fruit, vegetables, or bread crumbs. I also highly recommend buying some of the expandable freezer bags specially designed for storing soups and sauces—they stand up easily and have extremely strong zippers to prevent spillages. Having some of these instead of boxes of soups and sauces will save you lots of space.

Labeling

Buy strong labels designed to go in the freezer, which will prevent the frustration of trying to establish what's in a box at the bottom of the freezer when the label has dropped off! For bags, use a freezer marker pen (write on the bag before you fill it!). I tend to write what it is, how many portions, when it was made, and, if I need reminding, the use-by date.

Thawing frozen food

It is hard to be precise with thawing times, as it very much depends on the type of container you have frozen the food in—food in a thick metal container will take longer to defrost than food in a china or plastic one—and the quantity you have made. My suggestions are, therefore, just a guide. The safest place to thaw food is always in the fridge, where it will defrost slowly and remain cold once thawed. However, as a large container or casserole for eight could take up to two days to thaw in a very cold fridge, there is no harm in starting things off in a cool place for a few hours, then transferring it to the fridge to finish off. But make sure the place you choose is cool—don't leave food out to thaw in the height of summer near a window, especially if it contains meat, fish, dairy produce, or eggs! You can also use the microwave for defrosting and reheating, but just make sure it is piping hot and you eat it straight away.

USDA Advice

Cooking food from frozen

The United States Department of Agricultue advises that raw or cooked meat, poultry, or casseroles can be cooked or reheated from frozen but that it will take about one and a half times longer to cook than if cooked from a fully thawed state. It also recommends that when cooking whole frozen poultry, the giblet pack should be removed as soon as it can be loosened and the giblets cooked separately. The USDA also advises to look for the USDA or State inspection mark on food packaging, which indicates that the product has been prepared in a USDA or State-inspected plant under controlled conditions, and to follow the package directions for thawing, reheating, and storing. The USDA highlights the importance of checking the label on USDA-inspected frozen meat and poultry products because some of these, for example prestuffed whole birds, must be cooked from frozen to ensure they are safely cooked.

Freezing and refreezing food

The USDA advises that it is safe to refreeze previously frozen food that has been properly thawed in the fridge—although it warns of the possible loss in quality (see page 9)—as well as to freeze cooked foods previously frozen in their raw state. It also advises that frozen cooked foods properly thawed in the fridge can be refrozen but only the unused portion, that leftovers should be frozen within 3 to 4 days but that any foods left unrefrigerated for more than 2 hours, or 1 hour above 90°F, should not be refrozen.

Storage times

Here's a helpful guide to maximum storage times for freezer-friendly foods. Label and date things when you freeze them to prevent the risk of leaving foods in for too long (or they will lose their flavor). Remember, too, that the key to successful freezing is to wrap things well (see page 10).

Raw meat and fish

(Larger joints of meat will keep longer than smaller cuts.)

Bacon: 3 to 4 months
Beef: 8 to 12 months
Chicken: 8 to 12 months
Duck: 6 months
Game: 12 months
Lamb: 6 to 8 months
Ground meat: 3 to 4 months
Oily fish: 2 to 3 months
Pork: 4 to 6 months
Sausage: 3 to 4 months
Shrimp and scallops: 3 to 4 months
Smoked fish: 2 months
White fish: 4 months

Cooked foods

Baby purées: 2 months
Bread: 3 months
Butter: 6 months (best to freeze unsalted)
Cakes: 3 months
Casseroles, soups, and sauces: 3 months
Cheese, hard: 6 to 8 months
Cheese, soft: 3 months
Cooked meat (e.g. fully-cooked ham pieces): 1 to 2 months
Cookies and granola bars: 4 months
Cream: 3 months
Crêpes and Yorkshire puddings: 2 months
Eggs, raw, yolks/white: 12 months
Meringues and pavlovas: 1 month

Mousses, ice cream, and sherbet: 2 months
Pastry: 3 months
Stock: 6 months
Tarts, quiches, sausage rolls, and pies: 3 months

Fruits and vegetables

Apples, peeled, cored, and sliced: 4 to 6 months, open freeze slices, then bag
Asparagus, blanched: 12 months, cook from frozen
Beans, blanched: 6 to 8 months, cook from frozen
Butternut squash, raw: 12 months, open freeze, then bag, cook from frozen
Corn on the cob: 6 to 8 months, cook from frozen
French fries: up to 18 months
Herbs, fresh: 4 to 6 months
Rhubarb, raw, chopped: 12 months, cook from frozen
Seville oranges: 6 to 8 months
Stone fruit, halved and pitted: 12 months, unpitted: 3 months, cook from frozen
Summer berries: 12 months, open freeze (strawberries need to be puréed before freezing), thaw and use, or cook from frozen
Tomatoes, halved: 6 to 8 months, open freeze, then bag, use only for cooking, or grill/broil tomato halves

top leftovers to freeze

These suggestions for leftover food items to throw in the freezer and use at a later date have been accumulated by friends and family, all of whom have frozen leftovers with great success over the years!

Batter—for crêpes or Yorkshire puddings, for example (see pages 29 and 30), try freezing uncooked in small pots

Bread—turn day-old bread into crumbs (see page 23), then freeze in bags and use from frozen

Buttercream frosting

Canned tomatoes

Cheese—

  Hard cheese—can become more crumbly after freezing though, so use for crumbling into recipes, or shred prior to freezing, then freeze in bags and use from frozen

  Soft-rinded cheese, such as Brie or Camembert

Cooked vegetables—add to a pot of soup or mashed potatoes

Cream (not light)—good for sauces but not for whipping

Egg whites—freeze in pots or bags (make sure to note number of eggs), thaw, and use as fresh

Egg yolks—use an ice cube tray, sprinkle with salt or sugar, thaw, then use in sweet or savory recipes

Fruit juice

Gravy

Herbs—chop, then freeze (herbs that bruise, for example basil and tarragon, can be chopped and frozen in oil)

Homemade barbecue sauce

Lasagna or baked pasta—freeze leftovers as individual portions

Lemons, oranges, and limes—slice and open freeze on a tray before putting into a bag

Mashed potatoes

Meat juices from roasting chicken or turkey—pour off the fat and freeze the leftovers in cubes, thaw, then use to add to casseroles and gravies

Milk

Pasta or curry sauce from a jar

Pesto—freeze in ice cube trays

Pie dough

Roast chicken carcass—make stock at a later date

Roast meats, such as chicken or ham—shred or cube, then bag, thaw, and use

Wine—freeze in ice cube trays or pots and add frozen cubes to casseroles or sauces

what to make with gluts of fruit and vegetables

Even if you don't have a large vegetable patch, it's worth buying seasonal produce when it is at its cheapest and best and storing it for later months. Here's a list of ideas for ways to use various fruit and veg using recipes in the book (not including the baby purées in the final chapter).

Apples
Apple sauce (page 18)
Pork chops with mustard, apples and cider (page 72)
Healthier granola bars (page 106)
Christmas turnovers (page 146)
Various crumbles (page 148)

Eggplant
Eggplant and lentil moussaka (page 91)

Blackberries
Fruit puddings (page 136)
Late summer frangipane tart (page 144)
Blackberry and apple crumble (page 148)

Blueberries
Late summer frangipane tart (page 144)
Blue and red ice cream (page 128)
Blue and red terrine (page 130)

Broccoli
Fish pie with hidden vegetables (page 169)
Cauliflower and broccoli cheese with ham and tomatoes (page 166)

Butternut squash
Velvety butternut squash soup (page 48)
Coconut, chicken and butternut squash curry (page 66)

Carrots
Spicy carrot, tomato, chorizo and cilantro soup (page 43)
Velvety butternut squash soup (page 48)
Pork and flageolet bean stew (page 75)
Pork belly with crackling, fennel and shallots (page 76)
Slow-roast shoulder of lamb (page 92)
Smart shepherd's pie (page 93)

Cauliflower
Cauliflower and broccoli cheese with ham and tomatoes (page 166)

Celery
Watercress and pea soup (page 46)
Spicy carrot, tomato, chorizo and cilantro soup (page 43)
Ox cheeks with red wine and mushrooms (page 99)
Slow-roast shoulder of lamb (page 92)
Smart shepherd's pie (page 93)

Chillies
Thai green curry paste (page 37)

Zucchini
Zucchini and corn cakes (page 56)
Creamy zucchini, leek and Parmesan soup (page 44)
Pork and flageolet bean stew (page 75)
Eggplant and lentil moussaka (page 91)

Cucumber
Gazpacho (page 47)

Fennel

Fennel, leek and potato gratin (page 84)

Pork belly with crackling, fennel and shallots (page 76)

Leeks

Leek and blue cheese tartlets (page 58)

Creamy zucchini, leek and Parmesan soup (page 44)

Fennel, leek and potato gratin (page 84)

Peas

Watercress and pea soup (page 46)

Pears

Christmas turnovers (page 146)

Peppers

Gazpacho (page 47)

Sausages baked with puy lentils (page 74)

Portuguese seafood stew (page 68)

Potatoes

Fennel, leek and potato gratin (page 84)

Fish pie with hidden vegetables (page 169)

Smart shepherd's pie (page 93)

Eggplant and lentil moussaka (page 91)

Raspberries

Raspberry and white chocolate muffins (page 119)

Late summer frangipane tart (page 144)

Fruit cage puddings (page 136)

Pavlova with pomegranates and raspberries (page 134)

Summer berry crumble (page 148)

Redcurrants

Fruit cage puddings (page 136)

Rhubarb

Rhubarb crumble (page 148)

Rhubarb crunch ice cream (page 127)

Strawberries

Fruit cage puddings (page 136)

Pavlova with strawberries and passion fruit (page 135)

Summer berry crumble (page 148)

Strawberry and meringue ice cream (page 125)

Strawberry and rosewater vodka (page 137)

Corn

Zucchini and corn cakes (page 56)

Finnan Haddie chowder (page 51)

Tomatoes

All purpose-tomato sauce (page 33)

Tamarind and prawn parcels (page 61)

Gazpacho (page 47)

Spicy carrot, tomato, chorizo and cilantro soup (page 43)

Cauliflower and broccoli cheese with ham and tomatoes (page 166)

Watercress

Watercress and pea soup (page 46)

Smoked fish, crab and watercress tart (page 94)

basics
and batches

applesauce

$2^3/4$ pounds cooking apples, peeled and cored

This recipe is for a basic unsweetened purée, so it can be used in sweet and savory dishes. I often mix the purée with a can of apricots in juice and a sprinkle of sugar for a last-minute crumble filling. Or you can sweeten it a little and add it to softened onion, sage, and a little cream for a delicious accompaniment to pork. Timings do vary depending on the microwave, so don't treat those I've given as gospel!

Makes about 1 quart

Slice the apples fairly thinly and place in a saucepan or a microwave-safe dish. Add a dash of water, then cook over gentle heat, stirring occasionally, until the apples are soft. If you prefer, add a splash of water to the microwave-safe dish (about $1/2$ inch in the bottom) and cover with a lid or plastic wrap, pierced with one small steam hole. Microwave on high for 8 minutes. Stir the apples and return the dish to the microwave until the apples are soft, about 4 minutes. Purée if you prefer a completely smooth texture, or leave slightly chunky.

(F) Cool, then transfer to bags or pots, label, and freeze.

(D) Let stand for about 3 to 4 hours at room temperature or thaw in the microwave ("Defrost" setting).

(R) Place in a pan over low heat, or in a bowl in the microwave, until hot.

dark chocolate sauce

3/4 cup whole milk

2 tablespoons unsweetened cocoa

2 tablespoons golden syrup or dark
   corn syrup

4 tablespoons butter, diced

5$\frac{1}{2}$ ounces good-quality semisweet
   or bittersweet chocolate, broken
   into pieces

Ice cream and chocolate sauce is the most comforting no-work dessert, and a favorite of my father-in-law, which makes his visits easy! Try it over poached pears or crêpes, too, with a spoonful of cream.

Makes 1⅔ cups

In a saucepan, place a little of the milk with the cocoa and mix to a paste. Add the remaining milk and syrup and heat until nearly boiling. Remove the pan from the heat, let cool for a minute, then add the butter and chocolate and stir until melted.

(**F**) Pour the sauce into a container and cool, then cover, label, and freeze.

(**D**) Place the container in a bowl of hot water and stir occasionally, about 30 minutes, or thaw at room temperature.

(**R**) Spoon the sauce into a heatproof bowl and reheat over a pan of simmering water, or microwave with care.

Variation:

Rum and chocolate sauce—Stir in 1 to 2 tablespoons of rum before freezing.

white chocolate sauce

1$\frac{1}{4}$ cups heavy cream

10$\frac{1}{2}$ ounces good-quality white
   chocolate

about 1 tablespoon butter

This is a great sauce to serve hot poured over frozen summer berries.

Makes 1⅔ cups

In a heatproof bowl placed over a pan of barely simmering water, place all the ingredients and stir until the chocolate and butter have melted.

(**F**) Pour into a container, cool, then cover, label, and freeze.

(**D**) Place the container in a bowl of hot water and stir occasionally, about 30 minutes, or thaw at room temperature.

(**R**) Spoon the sauce into a heatproof bowl and reheat over a pan of simmering water, or microwave with care.

all-in-one white sauce

4 tablespoons butter
6 tablespoons all-purpose flour
2¹/₂ cups milk

I've converted to this simple white sauce purely because I'm always in a hurry and this is just as good as a traditionally made béchamel if it is to be used for a lasagna or cauliflower cheese. However, if, like my father, you prefer to make it the traditional way, then use the same quantities, but melt the butter, stir in the flour, and gradually incorporate the milk. This makes a thickish sauce, so just add more milk if you like it runnier.

Makes about 3 cups

In a saucepan, place all the ingredients over gentle heat and beat continuously. The butter will gradually melt and the sauce will then thicken. Use a spoon to scrape around the edge of the pan or you risk the sauce being lumpy. Bring to a boil, then season and simmer for 2 minutes.

(F) Pour into a container, place some plastic wrap over the surface of the sauce (to prevent a skin from forming), and let cool, then remove the plastic wrap, cover, label, and freeze.

(D) Can be defrosted at room temperature (if not too warm)—leave for 4 to 6 hours.

Variations:

Cheese sauce—Stir ²/₃ cup shredded cheese into the sauce as it simmers.

Parsley sauce—Melt the butter first and add 3 tablespoons chopped fresh parsley. Cook very gently for a minute or so, then stir in the flour and gradually incorporate the milk. Season with salt and pepper, bring to a boil, and simmer for 2 minutes.

Mushroom sauce—Sauté 6 sliced mushrooms in the butter, then add the flour and stir before gradually incorporating the milk. Season with salt and pepper, bring to a boil, and simmer for 2 minutes.

Shrimp sauce—Add a good handful of thawed cooked and peeled shrimp to the sauce once it has been defrosted and reheated. Simmer for 3 to 5 minutes or until piping hot. Do not refreeze.

bread sauce

scant 3 cups whole milk
$1/2$ onion
8 cloves
2 bay leaves
$2^1/4$ cups fresh white bread crumbs
about 2 tablespoons butter

Very simple to make, this rich and creamy sauce is an absolute must with roast chicken.

Makes about 3 cups (enough for 6 to 8 servings)

In a saucepan, place the milk and begin to heat gently. Meanwhile, stud the onion with the cloves and then add to the pan along with the bay leaves and some salt and pepper. Continue to heat as gently as you can until the milk is hot but not boiling. Add the bread crumbs, stir, and let gently simmer for 20 minutes. Remove the onion and bay leaves and transfer the sauce to a container or two.

(F) Cool, then cover, label, and freeze.

(D) Let stand overnight in the fridge (or put in the microwave on "defrost").

(R) Reheat gently in a pan, stirring in the butter just before serving.

bread crumbs

8 slices (about $10^1/2$ ounces) ready-sliced, day-old soft-crusted bread

Have these at the ready to coat strips of fresh chicken or fish, or for use in the above sauce.

Makes about 6½ cups

Break the bread into the bowl of a food processor and process until fine.

(F) Divide among 2 small bags. Label and freeze. There's generally no need to thaw before using.

madeira sauce

1 tablespoon butter
$^{1}/_{2}$ large onion, finely chopped
1 tablespoon all-purpose flour
3 thyme sprigs
1 bay leaf
1 cup beef consommé or beef stock
1 tablespoon red currant jelly
1 heaping teaspoon ketchup
6 tablespoons Madeira

This is a great freezer standby as it is the perfect accompaniment to beef or lamb and is a great help when you are making something that doesn't have juices for gravy, such as the Beef Wellington on page 80. This is a much-simplified version of a favorite recipe that my mother used to make to go with rack of lamb.

Makes about 1 cup

In a saucepan, melt the butter over gentle heat, add the onion, and sauté until softened, 5 to 10 minutes. Add the flour and stir, before adding the herbs, consommé or stock, red currant jelly, ketchup, and salt and pepper. Simmer for 10 minutes, then add the Madeira and simmer for an additional 5 to 10 minutes. Season to taste.

(F) Remove the herbs, then cool before freezing.

(D) Let stand at room temperature for about 4 to 6 hours.

(R) Warm gently in a pan.

chicken stock

2 roast chicken carcasses
2 celery stalks, chopped
1 large carrot, peeled and chopped
1 large onion, chopped
8 black peppercorns
few thyme sprigs
2 bay leaves
small bunch parsley,
    leaves and stems
$2^1/_2$ quarts cold water

I have to say I've never once made chicken stock from raw bones, but I do find making stock from a roast chicken carcass a pretty easy pastime: you can simply throw it into a pot and let it bubble away while you read the Sunday papers. The end result is wonderful and a lot cheaper than buying a carton of fresh chicken stock. Remember, though, that you'll need to add extra salt if you're using this stock as a replacement for a cube.

Makes about 1½ quarts

In a large pot, place all the ingredients and bring slowly to a boil, then simmer for about 2 hours. Strain through a strainer into pots or bags.

(F) Let cool before labeling and freezing.

(D) Let stand at room temperature for about 4 to 6 hours, depending on container size.

(R) Add to recipes as required.

sweet pie dough

Makes about 2¼ pounds

1 cup plus 2 tablespoons butter, softened
²/₃ cup superfine sugar
1 whole large egg plus 1 egg yolk
4 cups all-purpose flour, sifted
1 tablespoon cold water

In a food processor, cream the butter and sugar together. Add the eggs and blend again. Add the flour and water, blend for an additional 5 seconds, then scrape down the side of the bowl and blend again until all the ingredients are just combined and forming a lump. Bring the dough together using your hands and then weigh and divide it into portions of whatever size you like.

(F) Wrap tightly in a freezer bag and label, then freeze.

(D) Let stand at room temperature for about 1 to 2 hours. Use as needed.

pie dough

Makes about 1¾ pounds

4 cups all-purpose flour
¹/₂ cup plus 1 tablespoon butter, cold, cubed
¹/₂ cup plus 1 tablespoon shortening, cold, cubed
a good pinch of salt
ice-cold water

In a food processor, place the flour, fats, and salt. Pulse until crumb-like, then add water little by little until the mixture comes together. Bring the dough together using your hands. Roll out onto a floured counter, fold up, then divide into portions of whatever size you like.

(F) Wrap tightly in a freezer bag and label, then freeze.

(D) Let stand at room temperature for about 1 to 2 hours. Use as needed.

yorkshire puddings

3 large eggs
about $1^1/_3$ cups plus 1 tablespoon
   all-purpose flour
about $^3/_4$ cup lowfat milk or whole milk
   mixed with a little water
2 pinches sea salt flakes
sunflower or vegetable oil,
   for cooking

This is the easiest recipe ever! If you have only two eggs, then just measure their volume and use the same volume of flour and milk. Equally, you can double the batch and make more. If you remember when reheating them, a drizzle of roast beef drippings in the center of the Yorkshires makes them even more flavorsome.

Makes 12 to 14

You will need a 12 to 15-cup muffin pan.

Preheat the oven to 450°F. Crack the eggs into a measuring cup and measure their volume. Transfer to a bowl. Wash and dry the cup, then measure exactly the same volume of flour and sift into the bowl on top of the eggs. Pour the same volume of milk into the cup. Beat the eggs and flour together with the salt flakes and a grind of black pepper. Gradually beat in the milk. When the batter is smooth, pour it back into the measuring cup.

Pour about half a teaspoon oil into the bottom of each of the muffin cups. Place the pan in the oven to heat for 10 minutes. When the oil is scorchingly hot, pour the batter into each cup to about a third of the way up. Quickly put the pan back into the oven and bake for about 12 to 15 minutes, opening the door just at the end of the cooking time to check (they won't rise so well if you keep opening the door). Turn each pudding upside down in its cup and return the pan to the oven for an additional 2 minutes to crisp up the bottoms, then remove and turn the Yorkshires out onto a wire rack to cool.

(F) Open freeze, then transfer to a bag and label. You can also freeze the uncooked Yorkshire pudding mixture if you prefer (or have some left over), then thaw and cook as above.

(R) Cook from frozen for 5 to 10 minutes in a preheated hot oven (about 400°F). The temperature doesn't have to be exact, so you can simply put them in the oven as you are finishing off your roast.

custard sauce

1 cup whole milk

$1/3$ cup plus 1 tablespoon heavy cream

1 teaspoon best-quality vanilla extract with seed or 1 bean, scraped and seed added

2 large egg yolks

$1^1/_2$ tablespoons superfine sugar

1 heaping teaspoon cornstarch

I love custard sauce in every form. The recipe below is idiot proof and won't curdle, I promise! This makes quite a runny sauce; if you prefer yours thicker, then just add another teaspoon of cornstarch.

Makes about $1^2/_3$ cups

In a saucepan, place the milk and cream with the vanilla. Heat gently until hot but not boiling. Meanwhile, in a bowl, whip the eggs yolks, sugar, and cornstarch. Beat the hot milk and cream into the egg mixture to combine, then pour the mixture back into the pan and cook gently, stirring continuously, until the custard has thickened, about 3 to 4 minutes.

(**F**) Pour into a container and cover the surface with plastic wrap while it cools (to prevent a skin from forming). Remove the plastic wrap, cover, label, and freeze.

(**D**) Let stand overnight in the fridge.

(**R**) Warm gently in a pan.

crêpes

1 cup all-purpose flour

1 large egg

$1/2$ teaspoon vegetable or sunflower oil

pinch salt

$1^1/_4$ cups whole milk

about 2 tablespoons butter

Both the batter and the cooked crêpes are suitable for freezing.

Makes 6 crêpes

In a bowl or blender, place the flour, egg, oil, salt, and half the milk and beat or blend until smooth. Add the remaining milk and beat or blend again.

Melt a little of the butter and use a pastry brush to distribute a small amount evenly all over a crêpe pan or skillet. Add a ladleful of the batter and tip the pan around until it is evenly covered with a thin layer of the mixture. Cook over medium heat until beginning to brown. Use an offset spatula to turn the crêpe over (or flip it!). Cook the other side, then transfer to a sheet of wax paper. Repeat with the remaining mixture, layering each crêpe between sheets of wax paper.

(**F**) Wrap the package of cooled layered crêpes in foil and freeze.

(**D**) Let stand at room temperature for about 1 to 2 hours.

(**R**) Warm the package in a medium oven or in the microwave.

all-purpose tomato sauce

3 tablespoons olive oil
2 large red onions, finely chopped
$4^{1}/_{2}$ pounds fresh very ripe tomatoes
3 garlic cloves, crushed
2 teaspoons superfine sugar
$1^{1}/_{2}$ tablespoons balsamic vinegar

I've nicknamed this "glut of tomato sauce," as it used up all our homegrown tomatoes in one hit! I've kept the recipe simple and tasty, but it adapts well to the addition of some chile, carrot, zucchini, or freshly chopped basil. Tweak it as you wish and use it in pasta sauces, as a base for Bolognese, a topping for Pizza (see page 160), or a sauce for Chicken with Chorizo, Bell Peppers, and Olives (see page 84). The options are endless!

Makes abouts 1⅓ quarts

In a large saucepan, heat the oil gently, add the onions, and sauté very gently over low heat for 15 to 20 minutes. Meanwhile, in a large bowl, place the tomatoes and pour over boiling water to cover them. After a minute, drain off the water and slip off their skins (this really doesn't take long). Then coarsely chop them, discarding any tough cores.

Add the garlic and sugar to the onions and sauté for an additional 5 minutes, stirring occasionally. Add the tomatoes and their juices, balsamic vinegar, and some salt and pepper to the pan, then cook gently for 1 to $1^{1}/_{2}$ hours until the tomato sauce has thickened but is still a pourable consistency.

(F) Cool, divide among freezer containers or bags, cover, label, and freeze.

(D) Thaw at room temperature for about 4 to 5 hours, depending on quantity.

(R) Use in recipes or warm in a pan over low heat, or microwave.

ground beef for all occasions

3 to 4 tablespoons olive oil
$4^{1}/_{2}$ pounds good-quality ground beef
4 onions, chopped
6 large carrots, peeled and chopped
4 celery stalks, trimmed and sliced
4 garlic cloves, crushed
4 heaping teaspoons tomato paste
2 tablespoons all-purpose flour
3 bay leaves
4 teaspoons Worcestershire sauce
2 (14-ounce) cans diced tomatoes
1 quart beef stock

This is a sort of combination of Bolognese sauce and cottage pie filling. If you want to make the former, just add a squeeze of tomato paste and some mushrooms when reheating. If it's for cottage pie, simply reheat, adding some frozen peas if you like, and top with creamy root veg mash. You can also use this to make the Beef and Spinach Lasagna on page 98.

Makes 12 portions

In a large skillet, heat a tablespoon of the oil. Add about a third of the ground beef and, over high heat, cook until browned all over. Using a slotted spoon, remove the beef to a bowl. Cook the remaining beef in two batches, adding a little more oil to the pan as needed, removing to the bowl when browned.

Add the onions, carrots, and celery to the pan. Sauté gently, stirring occasionally, for about 10 minutes. Transfer the meat and vegetables to a large saucepan (or two if need be). Add the garlic, tomato paste, and flour and stir over the heat for an additional 2 minutes. Add the bay leaves, Worcestershire sauce, tomatoes, and stock. Stir, season with salt and black pepper, and simmer for 45 minutes, stirring occasionally.

(F) Cool, then divide into quantities required among lidded containers or bags, then label and freeze.

(D) Let stand overnight in the fridge.

(R) Use in recipes or warm in a pan over gentle heat.

chicken with white wine and herbs

8 chicken legs

3 bay leaves

1 teaspoon dried tarragon

15 black peppercorns

1-ounce bunch fresh parsley, leaves and stems separated

$3/4$ cup plus 1 tablespoon dry white wine

4 celery stalks, trimmed

4 medium onions, peeled

6 medium carrots, peeled

about 1 tablespoon butter

$3/4$ pound crimini mushrooms, quartered

2 garlic cloves, crushed

4 heaping tablespoons all-purpose flour

a dash of soy sauce

3 tablespoons heavy cream

My brother, Al, is an inspiring teacher at Jamie Oliver's cooking school, Recipease. This is an adaptation of one of his favorite recipes to enjoy at home. For a wonderful spring stew, try adding some blanched asparagus, peas, and beans, or top it with a crust for a comforting pie (see page 86).

Serves 8

In a large pot, place the chicken legs, bay leaves, tarragon, peppercorns, parsley stalks, white wine, and 2 celery stalks. Halve two of the onions and two of the carrots and add to the pan, then pour in enough cold water to cover the legs (about 2 quarts). Cover the pan and bring to a boil, then reduce to a simmer and cook, with the lid half on, for 25 minutes, or until juices in the legs run clear.

Remove the chicken legs from the pan and set aside, but keep the stock simmering. Meanwhile, chop the remaining onions, carrot, and celery into small chunks.

In a large saucepan over low heat, heat the butter, add the chopped vegetables and a pinch of salt, and sweat for 6 to 8 minutes. Meanwhile, strip the chicken from the bones and set aside. Place the bones, skin, and trimmings back in the simmering stock pot and continue to simmer.

Add the mushrooms and garlic to the pan with the chopped vegetables and turn up the heat to brown all the ingredients, 3 to 4 minutes. Stir in the flour and cook gently for a minute. Strain the stock into a measuring cup and measure out $3^1/3$ cups (you can freeze any extra). Add nearly all of the stock and the soy sauce to the pan of vegetables, stirring it in slowly until it comes back to a simmer and thickens. Add a little more stock if it is still too thick— it should be thick enough to coat the back of a spoon. Chop the parsley leaves and add to the pan, along with the chicken. Stir in the cream, then taste and adjust seasoning as needed.

(F) Pour into containers of the size you require (if you are making the Chicken, Ham, and Tarragon Pie on page 86 you will need to keep back about half). Let cool before covering, labeling, and freezing.

(D) Let stand overnight in the fridge.

(R) Place in a pan over gentle heat until piping hot.

thai green curry paste

8 kaffir lime leaves, shredded

4 shallots, sliced

4 green chiles, seeded and chopped into $1/2$-inch chunks

4 garlic cloves, chopped

2 lemongrass stalks, trimmed and finely chopped

1 (2-inch) piece fresh ginger, peeled and chopped

$2^3/4$-ounce bunch cilantro, stems and leaves

handful of basil leaves

$1^1/2$ teaspoons dark brown sugar or jaggery (palm sugar)

1 teaspoon sea salt flakes

1 teaspoon ground coriander

$3/4$ teaspoon Thai five-spice powder (optional)

2 tablespoons sunflower oil

2 tablespoons green peppercorns, drained

Whenever I had time, I always used to try and make my own Thai green curry paste instead of buying it in a jar. Now I just make a big batch and freeze it. It's infinitely better than store bought, and using a whole big bunch of herbs and piece of fresh ginger saves so much wastage. You can double this recipe if you want to make more. It's tricky to get the heat exactly right with chiles, as they vary enormously. It's up to you to decide whether you want to make a hotter version by including the seeds. You can use this paste to make Coconut, Chicken, and Butternut Squash Curry (page 66), Shrimp and Noodle Broth (page 71), or Asian Beef Skewers (page 62).

Makes 15 smallish cubes (enough for about 10 portions of curry)

In a food processor, place all the ingredients except the green peppercorns with 2 tablespoons water and process, scraping down the side of the bowl at intervals, until the mixture resembles a smooth paste. Transfer to a bowl and stir in the peppercorns.

(F) Spoon the sauce into an ice cube tray and freeze. Then transfer the curry paste cubes from the tray into a bag, label, and return to the freezer.

(R) Use three cubes for a two-serving curry. Heat a little oil in a pan, add the frozen cubes, and heat gently until thawed, then cook, stirring, for an additional 2 minutes before stirring in a can of coconut milk. Add your choice of chicken, shrimp, or vegetables, then, when cooked through, add a good dash of Thai fish sauce and a squeeze of lime juice.

garlic bread

4 tablespoons softened butter

2 garlic cloves

1 tablespoon chopped fresh parsley

1 large ciabatta or 14-ounce French loaf (best quality you can find), cut three-quarters of the way down into 1-inch-wide slices

It's rare that I buy garlic bread, and to be honest, unless you buy a "taste-how-expensive-this-is" version, the baguettes are, I find, a bit disappointing. However, good homemade garlic bread is a real treat and delicious as a casual appetizer before a bowl of pasta with friends.

Serves 4 to 6

In a bowl, mix the butter, garlic, and parsley and season with salt and pepper. Spread the insides of the loaf slices generously with the flavored butter.

(F) Wrap the ciabatta or loaf in foil, place in a plastic bag, and freeze.

(D) Remove from the freezer 2 to 3 hours before you need it.

(R) Preheat the oven to 425°F. Place the foil package on a baking sheet and bake for about 15 minutes until piping hot.

soups, appetizers, and nibbles

spicy carrot, tomato, chorizo, and cilantro soup

1 tablespoon olive oil

1 red onion, finely chopped

9 ounces cooking chorizo, skinned and chopped (these look like fresh sausage rather than salami)

14 ounces carrots, peeled and cut into small chunks

14 ounces sweet potatoes, peeled and cut into small chunks

3 celery stalks, trimmed and cut into small chunks

1 to 2 teaspoons dried red pepper flakes

1 teaspoon cumin seed

1/2 teaspoon ground coriander

1/2 teaspoon turmeric

2 cups chopped fresh tomatoes

1 quart chicken stock

1-ounce bunch fresh cilantro, chopped

1 (14-ounce) can chickpeas (garbanzo beans), drained

juice of 1 lime

To serve
wedges of bread and Manchego cheese (optional)

We have a small embarrassment in our house in that my husband has thus far produced nothing but knobbly carrots in his vegetable garden. We are told it's because we have stones in our soil, but as neither of us has the energy to rectify the problem by getting rid of the stones, I am stuck with misshapen, leggy carrots to cook with. This soupy stew is the answer and I feel happy that our rather ugly carrots now have the opportunity to shine!

Makes about 1¾ quarts

In a large pan, heat the oil and add the onion and chorizo. Sauté gently for 5 minutes, then add the carrots, sweet potato, and celery and cook for an additional 10 minutes, stirring occasionally. Add the spices and cook for 2 minutes, then add the tomatoes and stock. Season generously, bring to a boil, and simmer for 20 minutes, or until the vegetables are tender.

Transfer about four ladlefuls of soup to a blender and add half the cilantro and chickpeas. Purée the soup until smooth, then pour back into the pan with the remaining chickpeas, cilantro, and a good squeeze of lime. Stir together and taste for seasoning, adding more salt, pepper, or lime as needed. Serve with wedges of bread and some Manchego cheese if you like.

(F) Pour into a container, cool, label, and cover before freezing.

(D) Let stand overnight in the fridge.

(R) Place in a pan over low heat until hot.

creamy zucchini, leek, and parmesan soup

4 tablespoons butter

2 medium leeks, trimmed and sliced

3 celery stalks, trimmed and finely chopped

2 1/4 pounds zucchini, trimmed and thickly sliced

1 large garlic clove, chopped

2 rosemary sprigs

3 1/2 cups well-flavored chicken stock

3/4 cup grated Parmesan

1/3 cup sharp shredded cheddar

1 1/4 cups whole milk

To serve

2 tablespoons chopped fresh parsley

The great thing about this soup is that as long as you also include some regular-size zucchini, you can get rid of the large ones you are bound to grow at least one of each season! Remove the tough, seedy centers and peel of any larger zucchini before weighing—I use yellow squash, which tend to have softer skins that are OK to cook.

Serves 6

In a large saucepan, melt the butter and sauté the leeks and celery for 5 minutes. Add the zucchini and continue to cook for 10 minutes. Add the garlic and rosemary and stir over the heat for an additional 3 to 4 minutes. Pour in the stock, season, cover with a lid, and simmer until the vegetables are tender, about 15 minutes.

Remove the rosemary stems and stir in the cheeses, then the milk. Purée the soup and taste for seasoning. Serve scattered with the parsley.

(F) Pour into a container, cool, label, and cover before freezing.

(D) Let stand overnight in the fridge.

(R) Place in a pan over low heat until hot.

watercress and pea soup

2 tablespoons butter
1 large onion, sliced
2 celery stalks, trimmed and sliced
9 ounces potatoes, peeled and chopped
    into 2-inch cubes
$2^{1/3}$ cups chicken or vegetable stock
$1^{1/2}$ cups fresh or frozen peas
$5^{1/2}$ ounces watercress
2 cups whole milk

To serve
croutons and watercress sprigs
    (optional)

Living just next to watercress beds in Hampshire, southern England, I feel it's my duty to include at least one or two recipes that use this wonderfully nutritious leaf.

Makes about 1½ quarts

In a large saucepan, melt the butter, add the onion, and sauté gently for 6 to 8 minutes. Add the celery and potato and cook for an additional 5 minutes, stirring occasionally. Add the stock, bring to a boil, and then simmer for 15 minutes, or until the potato is tender.

Add the peas and watercress (reserving a few sprigs as garnish), bring to a simmer, stirring to wilt the watercress, and simmer for a couple of minutes. Turn off the heat, stir in the milk, then purée the soup in a blender or using a hand blender.

(F) Pour into a container, cool, cover, label, and freeze.

(D) Let stand overnight in the fridge.

(R) Pour into a pan and reheat gently. Ladle into bowls and serve garnished with crunchy croutons and watercress sprigs.

gazpacho

1/2 large cucumber, coarsely chopped
1 green bell pepper, seeded and cut
    into chunks
3 ripe vine tomatoes, cored and cut
    into wedges
1/2 small red onion, chopped
2 thick slices day-old white bread,
    torn into pieces
2 garlic cloves, chopped
2 1/2 tablespoons olive oil
2 1/2 tablespoons good-quality
    red wine or cider vinegar
pinch sugar
1 2/3 cups tomato juice
Tabasco sauce, to taste (optional)

This is great served really cold in shot glasses on a warm summer's evening. Alternatively, serve it in bowls with some cooked and peeled shrimp, drizzled with lemon and oil, or with some chopped blanched almonds sprinkled on top.

Makes 1 quart

In a bowl, place the cucumber, bell pepper, tomatoes, onion, bread, garlic, oil, vinegar, and sugar with some salt and pepper and stir together. Let stand for 4 hours or overnight for the flavors to infuse. Purée in a blender until completely smooth, then add the tomato juice and taste for seasoning, adding a splash of Tabasco if you like.

(F) Pour into a container, cover, label, and freeze.

(D) Let stand overnight in the fridge.

velvety butternut squash soup

4 tablespoons butter

1 large onion, peeled and chopped

$2^{1}/_{4}$ pounds butternut squash, peeled, seeded, and cut into chunks

2 large carrots, peeled and cut into chunks

$1^{1}/_{2}$ cups good-strength chicken stock

3 cups whole milk

pinch grated nutmeg

I'm fully aware that there are a million butternut squash soups out there, but I still think this one, with the addition of carrot, beats them all! Use a stand blender rather than a hand blender for a smoother soup.

Makes about 1¾ quarts

In a large saucepan, melt the butter, add the onion, and soften gently for 5 to 8 minutes while you prepare the other vegetables. Add the butternut squash and carrot and continue to cook gently for about 10 minutes, stirring occasionally. Pour the stock and milk into the pan and bring to a simmer, but do not boil. Let simmer for about 20 minutes, then season generously with salt, pepper, and nutmeg before puréeing in a blender and tasting for additional seasoning.

(F) Pour into a container, cool, label, and cover before freezing.

(D) Let stand overnight in the fridge.

(R) Place in a pan and reheat gently.

finnan haddie chowder

2 tablespoons butter
2 teaspoons olive oil
1 large onion, chopped
4 medium potatoes (each weighing
  about 6 ounces), unpeeled if new,
  and chopped into $^3/_4$–$1^1/_4$-inch cubes
1 tablespoon thyme leaves
splash of white wine
2 cups good-strength chicken stock
$3^1/_4$ cups whole milk
2 (7-ounce) cans corn kernels, drained,
  or 2 large corn on the cobs,
  kernels removed
1 pound undyed finnan haddie, cut into
  $1^1/_2$-inch chunks, or shelled clams

To serve
5 slices bacon
2 tablespoons heavy cream
handful of chives, snipped

Chowders are by far my favorite kinds of soup and often feature at our table for a Saturday lunch. The best, I think is clam, followed closely by finnan haddie. If you can, try and buy some really good-quality undyed finnan haddie, which has a more subtle flavor than some of the others.

Serves 4

In a large saucepan, heat the butter and oil, add the onion, and sauté over low heat for 5 minutes. Add the potatoes and cook for an additional 5 minutes. Add the thyme and wine and boil for a minute or so before pouring in the stock and stirring. Add the milk and bring to nearly boiling, then reduce the heat and simmer until the potatoes are almost tender, about 10 minutes.

Add the corn, finnan haddie, and a grinding of pepper and bring to a simmer. Let simmer until the haddock is just cooked, about 10 minutes. Taste for seasoning, adding a little salt if needed.

(F) Pour into a container, cool, label, and cover before freezing.

(D) Let stand overnight in the fridge.

(R) Pour into a pan and gently reheat, trying not to break up the fish.

(S) Heat a skillet and add the bacon. Pan-fry until crisp, then drain on paper towels. Ladle the soup into bowls and top each with a swirl of cream, some crispy bacon, and a sprinkle of chives.

sausage rolls with mustard and poppy seed

14 ounces good-quality herby sausages
all-purpose flour, for dusting
18 ounces homemade Pie Dough
   (see page 28) or store-bought all-
   butter pie dough, thawed if frozen
1 egg, beaten
2 to 3 tablespoons English or Dijon
   mustard, onion marmalade,
   or some chile jam if you prefer
poppy (or sesame) seed,
   for sprinkling

My mother has been making lovely crescent-shaped sausage rolls for years. She can't remember which entertaining book she originally found the recipe in, and I have changed it somewhat, but a big thank you to whoever came up with the idea of rolling them like a croissant! Don't scrimp on sausage meat inside or you will end up with a mouthful of pie crust! You can also use flavored sausage meat if you prefer.

Makes 18

Preheat the oven to 400°F.

Split the sausages using a sharp knife, then squeeze the sausage meat from the casings into a bowl. Divide into about 18 equal-size pieces. Roll each piece into a baby sausage shape (long and thin rather than dumpy!)

On a generously floured counter, roll out the pie dough thinly and trim the edges so that you have a square of about 13 inches x 13 inches. Cut the pastry lengthwise into three equal strips and cut each strip into three squares. Then cut each square in half diagonally so that you have 18 triangles.

Brush the edges of a dough triangle with egg, then place a small amount of mustard, onion marmalade, or chile jam and some sausage meat in the center. Roll the triangle up tightly toward the point, folding round the outer edges to seal. (Don't worry if you can still see a little of the sausage peeking through.) Brush all over with more egg and sprinkle with poppy or sesame seed. Repeat with the remaining triangles. Place all the sausage rolls on a baking sheet lined with wax paper and bake for 20 to 25 minutes.

(F) Cool, then freeze between sheets of wax paper in a box, or open freeze then place in a bag.

(R) Cook from frozen in a preheated oven at 400°F for about 8 minutes, or until piping hot.

two easy freezer pâtés

If I was organized enough, I'd always have a stash of these pâtés in the freezer. Rather like potted shrimp, another favorite, these little dishes are really useful for a Saturday lunch or a casual supper with friends.

Smoked trout pâté

Serves 4 to 6

$1/2$ cup plus 3 tablespoons butter
$4^{1}/_{2}$ ounces hot smoked trout fillets
$3^{1}/_{2}$ ounces smoked trout fillets
juice and zest of $1/2$ large lemon
5 tablespoons heavy cream
1 teaspoon anchovy sauce or 2 anchovy
   fillets in oil, drained and chopped

To serve

hot toast and lemon wedges

In a saucepan over low heat or in a bowl in the microwave, gently melt the butter, then cool for 5 minutes. Meanwhile, in a food processor, place the hot smoked trout fillets and half the smoked trout. Add the lemon juice and zest, cream, anchovy sauce or chopped anchovy fillets, and a good grinding of black pepper. Pour in three-quarters of the melted butter. Process, scraping down the side of the bowl once, until smooth. Tear up the remaining smoked trout and add to the food processor. Pulse until it is mixed in but the pâté is still a bit textured. Taste for seasoning, then divide among 4 to 6 jars (or spoon into one larger dish) and cover with the remaining butter. Chill.

Chicken liver parfait

Serves 6 to 8

1 cup plus 2 tablespoons butter
1 teaspoon vegetable oil
14 ounces fresh chicken livers,
   coarsely chopped if large
$1/2$ small onion, chopped
1 teaspoon fresh thyme leaves
2 fresh parsley stems
1 bay leaf
good splash of brandy, Madeira, or
   sweet sherry

To serve

hot toast, onion marmalade or
   chutney, and a squeeze of lemon

In a saucepan over low heat or in a bowl in the microwave, gently melt 5 tablespoons of the butter, then set aside. In a skillet, melt 5 tablespoons of the remaining butter with the oil. Add the onion and sauté until softened. Increase the heat, add the chicken livers, herbs, and a good seasoning of salt and pepper, and cook, stirring, for 3 to 4 minutes. Add the brandy, Madeira, or sherry and cook for an additional 2 minutes. Remove from the heat and cool slightly. Remove the bay leaf and any herb stems and blend the livers in a blender until smooth. Dice the remaining butter and, with the machine still running, add to the blender. Taste and adjust the seasoning if necessary.

If you want a very smooth pâté, pass the mixture through a strainer into a bowl. Spoon the pâté into individual pots or one large dish. Smooth the tops and gently pour the reserved melted butter over the top to cover. Chill.

(F) Cover the pots, then label and freeze.

(D) Let stand overnight in the fridge.

(S) Remove from the fridge up to an hour before serving so that it softens a little.

game terrine with pink peppercorns

4 tablespoons brandy

14 plumped pitted prunes

2 rabbits, boned (total boned weight about $1^3/_4$ pounds)

26 ounces pork belly slices, rind removed and chopped into $^1/_2$–$^3/_4$-inch chunks

about 1 tablespoon butter

splash of vegetable oil

1 small onion, chopped

2 rabbit livers

2 garlic cloves, chopped

$3^1/_2$ ounces cubed pancetta

$^1/_2$ teaspoon ground allspice

$^1/_2$ teaspoon thyme leaves

2 eggs, beaten

6 tablespoons good-quality chicken stock

2 teaspoons sea salt flakes

2 teaspoons pink peppercorns in brine, drained

$10^1/_2$ ounces or about 12 slices smoked bacon

To serve

hot toast, arugula salad, and cornichons

If you aren't a fan of rabbit, pheasant or chicken also work well.

Makes 2 (2-pound) loaves, each serving 8 to 10

You will need 2 (2-pound) loaf pans.

In a small bowl, place half the brandy and all the prunes and let soak. Preheat the oven to 350°F.

Set aside about half the boned rabbit to use in the middle of the terrine. Choose the loin fillets for this, plus a little extra of the remaining meat if needed, and cut into long, fairly thick strips. Cut the remaining meat into smallish pieces and place in a bowl with the chopped pork belly.

In a skillet, melt the butter with the oil and sauté the onion until softened, 5 to 8 minutes. Add the livers and garlic and pan-fry, stirring, until sealed. Add the remaining brandy and cook for an additional 2 minutes, then transfer to the bowl of pork and rabbit, along with the pancetta, allspice, thyme, eggs, stock, salt, and a good grinding of pepper. Stir together, then transfer to a food processor in batches (depending on the size and strength of your appliance) and process until it has a chunky ground texture—it should not be smooth. Transfer back to the bowl and stir in the pink peppercorns.

Line the 2 loaf pans with the bacon slices, laying them side by side across the pan, with their ends hanging over the sides. Spoon half the mixture into the pans and lay the prunes in a line lengthwise down the center. Put the whole pieces of rabbit next to the prunes, filling all the remaining space, then top with the remaining mixture and lay the bacon ends over the top. Wrap each pan completely in foil, then sit them in a roasting pan. Fill three-quarters of the way up with boiling water, then bake the terrines for $1^1/_2$ hours.

Remove from the oven and cool, then wrap the loaf pans in plastic wrap, place weights on top (cans or scales weights would be perfect for this), and refrigerate overnight.

(F) Remove the terrines from their pans, clean off any jelly from the outside, wrap in plastic wrap and foil, and freeze.

(D) Let stand overnight in the fridge.

(S) Remove from the fridge up to an hour before serving. Slice the terrines and serve with hot toast, arugula salad, and cornichons.

zucchini and corn cakes with smoked salmon

1²/₃ cups all-purpose flour

1 tablespoon baking powder

2 large eggs, beaten

1 heaping teaspoon sea salt flakes

3 pinches cayenne pepper

1¹/₂ tablespoons snipped chives

³/₄ cup whole milk

2 tablespoons butter, melted, plus about 1 tablespoon for pan-frying

6 ounces zucchini, trimmed and shredded

2 (3¹/₂-ounce) corn on the cobs, cooked and kernels removed, or 5¹/₂ ounces canned corn kernels, drained

To serve

7 ounces smoked salmon

8 tablespoons crème fraîche or sour cream

¹/₂ small red onion, very thinly sliced

baby capers, snipped chives, and lemon wedges

These were on the menu at a restaurant where I worked in Port Douglas, Australia. They also make a delicious alternative to blinis if you make them canapé sized.

Makes 8 cakes (1 per person as an appetizer)

In a bowl, place the flour, baking powder, eggs, salt, cayenne pepper, and chives. Add the milk, melted butter, and a good grinding of pepper and beat with a whip. Add the zucchini and corn kernels and stir.

In a large skillet, melt the remaining butter and spoon in the zucchini mix, about 1¹/₂ tablespoons per cake, to make three cakes in the pan (they should be quite thick). Pan-fry gently until golden, about 5 minutes, then turn them over and cook the other sides.

(F) Transfer the cakes to wax paper sheets and freeze.

(D) Place on a baking sheet and let stand for 2 hours at room temperature.

(R) Preheat the oven to 325°F. Put the baking sheet into the oven for 10 to 15 minutes, or until the cakes are hot.

(S) Place the cakes on plates and top each with a mound of smoked salmon, a good spoonful of crème fraîche or sour cream, some thinly sliced red onion, capers, and snipped chives. Serve with lemon wedges.

leek and blue cheese tarts

14 ounces homemade Pie Dough (see page 28) or 1 (14-ounce) box refrigerated ready-rolled pie crust

2 tablespoons butter

3 medium leeks, trimmed and finely chopped

2 eggs and 1 egg yolk

1 cup heavy cream

1 heaping cup crumbled blue cheese, such as Stilton

To serve
dressed salad greens

These are appetizer-size, but feel free to make them smaller or larger if you like. There are lots of other versions you can make with the same egg mix poured over—bacon and pea, caramelized onion, or broccoli to give you just a few ideas.

Makes 6

You will need 6 small loose-bottom tart pans about $4\frac{1}{2}$ to 5 inches in diameter and dried beans.

On a floured counter, roll out the pie dough until really thin. (Even ready-rolled pastry benefits from being a little bit thinner, as you then get a crisp bottom and a better filling to crust ratio.) Cut out circles from the dough to line your tart pan and prick the bottoms. Cut circles of wax paper large enough to line each tart shell. Scrunch up the paper circles, then open them up again, place inside the tart pans and fill with dried beans. Place the tart pans on a cookie sheet and bake for 5 minutes, then remove the beans and paper and dry out in the oven for an additional 5 minutes or so.

Meanwhile, in a saucepan, heat the butter and sauté the leeks very gently until softened, about 10 minutes, stirring occasionally. In a bowl, beat the eggs and the cream with some seasoning.

Remove the tarts from the oven and divide the leeks among them, then top with the crumbled blue cheese. Finally, pour in the egg mix until it reaches the top of each tart shell. Bake for about 15 to 20 minutes, or until risen and golden. Remove from the oven and let cool.

(F) When cool, remove the tarts from the pans and open freeze. Then wrap in foil or place in a container, cover, and label.

(R) Place the frozen tarts on a baking sheet and bake at 350°F for 15 to 20 minutes until piping hot. (Cover with foil if necessary to prevent them from becoming too brown.)

This also works in a larger $9\frac{1}{2}$-inch diameter, 1-inch deep quiche pan. Cook for 30 minutes and reheat from frozen covered with foil at 350°F for 45 to 55 minutes, or until piping hot.

tamarind and shrimp triangles

2 teaspoons vegetable oil

1 onion, finely chopped

1 garlic clove, crushed

1-inch piece fresh ginger, peeled and chopped

$1/2$ large red chile, seeded and chopped

14 cherry tomatoes, halved

2 tablespoons tamarind pulp

juice of $1/2$ lime

$1^1/2$ teaspoons Thai fish sauce

2 tablespoons chopped fresh cilantro

8 ounces raw peeled jumbo shrimp, chopped into $5/8$-inch chunks

6 sheets frozen phyllo dough, thawed

5 tablespoons butter, melted, plus 4 tablespoons for brushing dough once thawed

To serve

salad greens and mango chutney

Make these as an appetizer, or smaller versions for canapés. They are delicious served warm from the oven with a few salad greens on the side and maybe some mango chutney for dipping. Keep the seeds in the chile if you want a more fiery end result.

Makes 12 triangles (serves 6 as an appetizer)

In a pan, heat the oil and gently sauté the onion until softened, about 10 minutes. Add the garlic, ginger, and chile and sauté for 2 to 3 minutes. Then add the tomatoes, tamarind, and lime and cook until the tomatoes are soft, about 10 minutes. Stir in the fish sauce, remove the pan from the heat, and let cool.

When completely cool, stir in the cilantro and shrimp.

Lay the sheets of phyllo out on a clean counter and cover with a damp dish towel. Take one phyllo sheet and brush all over with the melted butter. Taking hold of one long side, fold it toward the center. Brush again with the melted butter and fold in the other side to make a long, triple-layered strip. Cut this in half so that you have two pieces about 8 inches long and $3^1/4$ inches wide.

Place 2 teaspoons of the filling at one end of the strip, leaving a $3/4$-inch border. Take the right corner and fold diagonally to the left, enclosing the filling and forming a triangle. Fold again along the upper crease of the triangle. Keep folding in this way until you reach the end of the strip. Place the triangle on a baking sheet covered in wax paper. Continue until you have made all 12 triangles.

(F) Open freeze the unbaked triangles, then transfer to a container, label, and cover.

(C) Brush the frozen triangles with melted butter, then bake at 400°F for 25 minutes, or until golden. Serve with salad greens and mango chutney (loosen with a little hot water).

asian beef skewers

25 ounces good-quality beef sirloin
 steak, sliced into $2^3/_4$-inch strips
vegetable oil, for brushing

For the spicy marinade
1-inch piece fresh ginger, peeled and
 finely chopped
1 large garlic clove, finely chopped
1 red chile, seeded and finely chopped
1 lemongrass stalk, trimmed and very
 finely chopped
2 tablespoons soy sauce
$1^1/_2$ tablespoons Thai fish sauce
2 teaspoons sesame oil

To serve
Asian-style salad made from
 cucumber ribbons, sliced scallions,
 and cilantro leaves.
sweet chili or satay sauce, for dipping

This recipe also works marinated with the Thai Green Curry Paste (see page 37) mixed with a little coconut milk. These are great for the barbecue, too.

Makes 12 skewers (serves 6 as an appetizer)

You will need 12 wooden or metal skewers.

In a bowl, place all the marinade ingredients and stir together. Add the steak and mix well. Cover the bowl and place in the fridge to marinate for 1 hour. Remove the meat strips from the marinade and thread onto skewers.

(F) Lay a freezer bag on a plate and put the skewers inside, lying them side by side. Freeze, then remove the plate from underneath and tie the bag.

(D) Let thaw thoroughly overnight.

(R) When ready to cook, heat a large grill pan until smoking hot. Brush the skewers with a little vegetable oil, then chargrill the skewers, turning occasionally and pushing down on them with a spatula, for a total of about 4 to 5 minutes, until cooked through as you like. Serve with the Asian-style salad and sweet chili or satay sauce for dipping.

spicy lamb kabobs

For the kabob
18 ounces ground lamb
1 teaspoon ground cumin
$1/_2$ teaspoon ground coriander
$3/_4$ teaspoon hot chili powder
$1/_2$ teaspoon dried oregano
1 teaspoon fresh thyme leaves

To serve
6 flatbreads or pita bread
1 cup plain yogurt
$1/_2$ cucumber, halved lengthwise,
 seeded, and shredded
1 small garlic clove, crushed
seeds of 1 pomegranate
$1/_2$ red onion, finely sliced
handful of fresh mint leaves, chopped
lime wedges

You can cook the kabobs on the barbecue if you like.

Serves 6

In a bowl, combine the kabob ingredients with 1 teaspoon sea salt and a good grinding of black pepper. Mix well until thoroughly combined. Divide into six equal portions and form each into a sausage shape around a kabob stick.

(F) Put the kabobs into a freezer bag, lying them side by side. Freeze on a plate, then remove the plate from underneath and tie the bag.

(D) Let stand in the fridge for 4 to 5 hours.

(S) Broil the kabobs for 10 minutes, turning, until cooked through and browned. Meanwhile, warm the flatbreads. Mix the yogurt with the cucumber, garlic, and some salt and pepper. Serve the kabobs with the warmed flatbreads or pita bread, the cucumber and yogurt sauce, red onion, mint leaves, pomegranate seeds, and lime wedges.

meals using frozen ingredients

There are many bags of meat, poultry, and seafood available in supermarkets that specify "can be cooked from frozen," and with our "no time but want to cook" attitude to preparing meals nowadays, they are exactly what we need. They are easy and safe to use, and there are no extras added—they have just been blast frozen as individual pieces and you simply cook them a little longer than you would fresh. Fingers crossed there are more to come—particularly good-quality meat and free-range poultry.

If you prefer, of course, you can freeze your own meat in easily removable packaging—hamburgers, sausage, and chops are just some of the things that can be cooked from frozen—and I have found the plus side to buying and freezing your own meat is that you can choose the best quality. Freeze items individually—flat, or side by side, rather than in a lump—otherwise you will find it tricky to ensure they cook evenly and, most importantly, the whole way through. Wrap them tightly and you'll avoid freezer burn. Even better, ask your friendly butcher to pack your meat in sizes you require and then vacuum pack it.

The recipes in this chapter all use meat or seafood that can be cooked from frozen, but you can also make them using fresh meat or seafood—just reduce the cooking time a little. All these dishes are also suitable for freezing once cooked. Just make sure you thaw them in the fridge overnight and reheat until piping hot.

coconut, chicken, and butternut squash curry

1 tablespoon sesame oil

3 cubes frozen Thai Green Curry Paste (see page 37) or 2 tablespoons from a jar

$1/2$ teaspoon ground coriander

$1/2$ teaspoon turmeric

14 ounces frozen chicken chunks (or fresh chicken if you prefer)

1 (14-ounce) can coconut milk

$10^1/2$ ounces frozen or fresh butternut squash chunks

2 ripe tomatoes, chopped, or a handful of cherry tomatoes

1 (8-ounce) can bamboo shoots, drained and rinsed (optional)

2 tablespoons Thai fish sauce

good squeeze of lime or lemon juice

To serve

basmati rice

1 tablespoon chopped fresh cilantro (optional)

The ultimate modern, quick meal—and yes, you really can add frozen chicken and butternut to this! Just make sure you buy chicken that has been frozen in similar-size individual chunks, as this will ensure even cooking. You can use raw frozen shrimp instead of chicken if you prefer. If you have any left over, you can freeze, thaw, and reheat at another time.

Serves 2 to 3

In a pan, heat the sesame oil, add the curry paste, and gently cook until thawed (or add the store-bought paste to the pan and stir-fry for a minute). Add the ground coriander and turmeric and cook over medium heat for 1 to 2 minutes. Add the frozen chicken chunks and half the can of coconut milk and bring to a boil, then reduce the heat and simmer for 10 minutes.

Add the butternut squash, tomatoes, and the remaining coconut milk and bring back up to a boil. Reduce the heat to a simmer and continue cooking until the squash is tender and the chicken is cooked through and piping hot, an additional 10 to 15 minutes. If using, add the bamboo shoots for the final 5 minutes of cooking time. Stir in the fish sauce and lime or lemon juice, to taste. Serve with basmati rice, garnished with chopped cilantro, if using.

portuguese seafood stew

1 tablespoon olive oil

1 red onion, cut into wedges, or
   3 handfuls of chopped frozen onion

2 bell peppers, seeded and cut into
   chunks (or frozen bell pepper
   slices—add with the strained
   tomatoes)

14 ounces new potatoes, cut into
   smallish chunks

1 to 2 pinches dried red pepper flakes

2 bay leaves

splash of white wine

$^1/_2$ (24-ounce) jar of strained tomatoes
   with garlic and onions

$1^1/_4$ cups chicken or vegetable stock

1 (14-ounce) bag frozen mixed
   seafood (raw calamari rings, shrimp,
   mussels, and scallops) or 14 ounces
   fresh mixed seafood

handful of chopped fresh parsley
   (optional)

To serve
garlic bread or salad

Based on traditional Cataplana, this recipe uses a bag of cook-from-frozen seafood, so makes a simple quick dinner. Serve it with garlic bread or a big salad.

Serves 4

In a wok or large pan, heat the oil, add the onion and bell peppers, and sauté for 5 minutes over medium heat. Add the potatoes and sauté for an additional 7 minutes. Stir in the red pepper flakes, bay leaves, and wine, then add the strained tomatoes and stock, stir, and bring to a boil. Reduce the heat and simmer for 15 minutes.

Add the frozen seafood and continue cooking until the potatoes are tender and the seafood is cooked through and piping hot, 8 to 10 minutes. Add the parsley (if using) and serve.

fish pot pies

1 (14-ounce) box ready-rolled puff
    pastry, thawed if frozen
milk, for brushing
2 eggs
about 1 tablespoon butter
splash of oil
1 onion, finely chopped, or 3 good
    handfuls of frozen chopped onions
6 mushrooms, quartered
24 ounces store-bought cheese sauce
    or 1 quantity Cheese Sauce
    (see page 22), thawed if frozen
$1\frac{1}{2}$ teaspoons Dijon mustard
$1\frac{3}{4}$ pounds frozen mixed smoked and
    unsmoked skinless fish fillets, cut
    into chunks, or use fresh
7 ounces frozen medium shrimp
2 teaspoons baby capers (optional)
2 heaping tablespoons chopped
    fresh parsley

I love those individual one-pot pies you often see, but, I don't know about you, I never have enough suitable ovenproof bowls or dishes to serve them in. So for this I've cheated! Choose any pretty bowls or dishes, as long as they can be warmed. If using frozen, take the pastry and cheese sauce out of the freezer in the morning, but you can cook the fish and shrimp direct from frozen and you'll be able to create a smart fish pie with barely the flick of a wooden spoon! Buy separate bags of frozen smoked and unsmoked fish and shrimp, and measure out what you need.

Serves 4 to 6, depending on the size of your dishes

Preheat the oven to 425°F. Unroll the pastry and cut 4 to 6 circles or interesting shapes to sit on top of your bowls. Grease a baking sheet or cut a rectangle of wax paper to line your sheet. Transfer the shapes to your prepared sheet and score each with a crisscross pattern. Brush with milk and bake for 12 to 15 minutes, then remove and keep warm.

Meanwhile, boil the eggs for 6 to 8 minutes and make the sauce. In a pan, heat the butter and oil until the butter has melted, then add the onion and soften over low heat, 3 to 4 minutes. Add the mushrooms and sauté for 2 to 3 minutes. Add the cheese sauce, mustard, and some ground black pepper and bring to a simmer. Stir in the frozen fish and shrimp and gently simmer for about 10 minutes, stirring carefully occasionally.

Drain the eggs, rinse in cold water, then peel and cut into pieces. Add to the fish, along with the capers (if using) and parsley. When the fish is cooked and piping hot, divide it among the dishes and top each with a puff pastry shape.

shrimp and noodle broth

2 tablespoons flavorless oil, such as
   peanut or sunflower
2 cubes frozen Thai Green Curry Paste
   (see page 37) or 1 heaping tablespoon
   from a jar
5 button or shiitake mushrooms,
   quartered (or 2 handfuls frozen
   mushroom slices)
$1^2/_3$ cups good-quality chicken stock
$5^1/_2$ ounces raw frozen shrimp (look for
   a bag that says "cook from frozen")
2 handfuls of mixed stir-fry vegetables,
   such as baby corn, snow peas or
   sugar snap peas, and bell pepper,
   or frozen stir-fry vegetable mix
1 tablespoon Thai fish sauce
juice of 1 lime
6 ounces ready-cooked rice noodles
2 scallions, sliced

Nothing beats this soup when you are on a bit of a health kick, or are just in the mood for something light. Fragrant and full of crunchy vegetables, it's a real pick-me-up. Buy dried noodles and cook according to the package directions if you prefer.

Serves 2

In a pan, heat the oil, add the curry paste, and gently cook until thawed (or add the store-bought paste to the pan and stir-fry for a minute). Add the mushrooms and sauté for 2 minutes. Add the chicken stock and heat until simmering, then stir in the shrimp. Once the broth has come back to a boil, throw in the mixed vegetables. Cook until the shrimp are cooked through and piping hot, 3 to 5 minutes. Stir in the fish sauce and lime juice.

Reheat the noodles following the package directions and divide among two bowls. Ladle over the soup and garnish with the scallions .

pork chops with mustard, apples, and cider

1 tablespoon olive oil

about 2 tablespoons butter

4 (7-ounce) bone-in thick pork chops, frozen (or fresh, if you prefer)

1 small onion, chopped, or 2 handfuls of frozen chopped onion

9 ounces frozen baking apple slices or peeled and sliced fresh baking apple

2 garlic cloves, chopped

8 sage leaves

1 cup dry hard cider

$1\frac{1}{2}$ heaping tablespoons grainy mustard

1 cup chicken stock

2 tablespoons heavy cream (optional)

To serve

baked potatoes

Using frozen chops in a braised dish like this one is no different from using fresh, as you are tenderizing the pork in the hard cider and apple sauce, so the chops have no chance of drying out. Just make sure the chops are not frozen in a lump. If you have any left over, you can freeze, thaw, and reheat on another occasion.

Serves 4

Preheat the oven to 325°F. In a skillet, heat the oil and 1 tablespoon of the butter and pan-fry the frozen pork chops over high heat until browned (about 5 minutes on each side). Season and transfer to a casserole dish.

Add the remaining tablespoon of butter to the pan and, once melted, add the onions and cook, stirring, for 5 minutes. Add the apple slices, garlic, and sage and cook, stirring, for an additional 2 to 3 minutes. Transfer the pan contents to the casserole dish.

Add the hard cider to the pan and bring to a boil, scraping the base of the pan to incorporate all the lovely flavors. Add the mustard and stir together, then pour over the pork and apples, along with the stock. Cover with a lid and bake in the oven for $1\frac{1}{2}$ hours.

Remove the pork chops to a baking dish and keep warm. Place the casserole dish over medium heat and let the gravy bubble for 5 minutes or so to reduce and concentrate it. Stir in the cream, if using, season to taste, and serve with the chops and some baked potatoes.

asparagus and pea risotto

about 1 tablespoon butter, plus
    2 tablespoons to stir in at the end
2 teaspoons olive oil
$^1\!/_2$ onion, chopped, or 2 handfuls
    frozen chopped onions
4 mushrooms, quartered, or a large
    handful of frozen mushroom slices
1 garlic clove
1 cup carnaroli rice (or other risotto
    rice, e.g. arborio)
splash of white wine (optional)
$2^1\!/_2$–3 cups hot vegetable stock
$^3\!/_4$ cup frozen peas
$5^1\!/_2$ ounces frozen or fresh asparagus
    spears, snapped in half
2 tablespoons grated Parmesan cheese

Risotto is such a brilliant midweek standby, as you can adapt it to suit the contents of your fridge (or freezer) and this one is very colorful as well as being healthy, too. Add chicken or shrimp to this for a non-veggie version. You can also use some frozen baby fava beans if you are not in possession of any asparagus, or use fresh if in season.

Serves 2 to 3

In a deep skillet or sauté pan, heat the tablespoon butter and add the onion. Sauté gently, stirring, for 3 to 4 minutes, then add the mushrooms and garlic and cook for a minute or two. Add the rice and cook, stirring, for an additional 2 minutes, then pour in the wine, if using, or a ladleful of stock and stir until absorbed. Keep adding the stock, about $^3\!/_4$ cup at a time, letting it bubble and stirring at intervals until it is absorbed by the rice.

When you have only about $^3\!/_4$ cup stock left to add, test the rice. If it still has a crunch to it, add a bit more stock and cook gently for a little longer. Add the peas and asparagus with the final addition of stock. Let the vegetables cook for a couple of minutes, then remove the pan from the heat. The risotto should be creamy and silky, neither too soupy nor too dry (add a bit more stock if necessary). Season, then stir in the grated Parmesan and the butter. Let the risotto rest for 5 minutes before ladling it into bowls.

sausage baked with puy lentils

12 frozen or fresh sausages
2 red bell peppers, seeded and thickly
    sliced, or 2 handfuls frozen bell
    pepper slices
2 red onions, cut into wedges
2 tablespoons olive oil
1 quart hot beef stock
1 tablespoon Dijon mustard

Buy really good-quality butcher's or specialty sausage for this dish, not the commercial frozen kind—frozen venison works really well, as do some of the more spicy varieties now available. Package them side by side on a tray or just open freeze the individual sausages and take them out as you need them. If you've got thawed sausage to hand, simply reduce the browning time at the beginning.

Serves 4 to 6

1 teaspoon English mustard powder

1½ tablespoons tomato paste

2 garlic cloves, crushed

heaping 1 cup dry Puy lentils

2 rosemary sprigs

2 bay leaves

Preheat the oven to 350°F.

In a medium roasting pan, arrange the sausages in a single layer and bake for 35 minutes until lightly browned (if cooking from fresh they will take a little less time). Remove the pan from the oven and add the bell peppers, onion, and oil. Toss together, then return to the oven for 10 minutes.

In a pitcher, mix the hot stock with the mustards, tomato paste, garlic, and a good grinding of black pepper. Scatter the lentils over the sausage, then add the herbs and pour over the stock mixture. Stir and then bake uncovered for 35 to 40 minutes, turning the sausage and lentils over in the juices halfway through the cooking time.

pork and flageolet bean stew

Another winning dish that involves minimal preparation while giving the impression that it has taken ages! The frozen pork needs to be in individual pieces otherwise it won't cook evenly from frozen, so either buy the "cook from frozen" bags or open freeze your pork chunks on a tray before bagging them up. If you prefer you can make this dish using fresh pork. Any leftovers can be frozen, thawed, and reheated at another time.

Serves 4

1 tablespoon vegetable oil

1 large onion, cut into wedges, or 3 good handfuls of frozen chopped onion

1 pound frozen cubes of pork leg, or fresh pork, cut into bite-size pieces

1½-inch piece fresh ginger, peeled and chopped

1 large garlic clove, chopped

3 carrots, peeled and chopped

1 medium baking apple, peeled, cored, and sliced, or a handful of frozen apple slices

heaping ⅓ cup white wine

1 tablespoon Worcestershire sauce

3 tablespoons honey

1 tablespoon soy sauce

1¼ cups vegetable stock

6 mushrooms, sliced, or 2 handfuls frozen mushroom slices

1 (14-ounce) can flageolet beans, drained and rinsed

1 medium zucchini, trimmed and sliced

Preheat the oven to 300°F. In a heavy-bottom casserole dish, heat the oil and add the onion. Soften over medium heat for 5 minutes. Increase the heat and add the pork. Cook, stirring, for 5 minutes, then add the ginger, garlic, carrot, and apple and cook, stirring, for an additional 5 minutes. Add the wine, Worcestershire sauce, honey, soy sauce, and vegetable stock. Season, stir, bring to a boil, and then cover and cook in the oven for an hour.

Remove the casserole from the oven and add the mushrooms, beans, and zucchini. Stir, cover the casserole, and return to the oven for an additional 30 minutes, or until the pork is tender. Taste for seasoning and sweetness, then serve.

pork belly with cracklings, fennel, and shallots

1 piece boneless pork belly, weighing about 4 pounds once boned (about 5 pounds pre-boned weight), skin scored, frozen in a flat piece

3 heaping teaspoons sea salt flakes

1 teaspoon fennel seeds

zest of 1 lemon

$1\frac{1}{2}$ cups dry hard cider, plus a splash for the gravy

1 large fennel bulb, trimmed, cored, and cut into wedges

5 medium carrots, peeled and halved or quartered lengthwise

12 shallots, peeled

3 garlic cloves, unpeeled but squashed with the back of a knife

$1\frac{1}{4}$–$1\frac{2}{3}$ cups chicken stock

For the gravy

3 teaspoons honey

2 teaspoons soy sauce

To serve

steamed cabbage

mashed potatoes

Applesauce (see page 18)

Wonderful pork belly has got everything, as long as it's cooked slowly: tender meat with lots of flavor and crispy cracklings. And cooking it from frozen is just brilliant! However, if cooking from fresh, just spread it with the lemony mixture before it goes in the oven, keep it skin side up from the start, and omit the initial cooking at the high temperature.

Serves 4 to 6

Preheat the oven to 450°F.

Lay the pork belly skin side down on a roasting rack inside a large roasting pan. Roast for 25 minutes on the top rack of the oven. Meanwhile, using a mortar and pestle, pound half the salt with the fennel seeds, lemon zest, and a good grinding of black pepper. Remove the pork from the oven and rub the lemony mixture all over the flesh. Carefully turn the meat over so that it is skin side up and sprinkle over the rest of the salt, using the back of a spoon to rub it into the skin. Reduce the oven to 300°F, pour the hard cider into the base of the roasting pan—not over the meat, or you won't get cracklings—and return it to the oven, on the center rack, for 1 hour.

Add the vegetables and garlic to the bottom of the pan under the pork. Pour in $1\frac{1}{4}$ cups stock (avoiding the meat again) and cook for an additional $1\frac{3}{4}$ hours, or until the vegetables are just tender. Check occasionally to make sure there is enough liquid, adding more stock if necessary.

Remove the pan from the oven and increase the heat to 450°F. Take the pork and roasting rack out of the pan, sit it on another roasting pan, and return to the oven for 20 to 30 minutes. (Then, if the cracklings still haven't developed, simply remove the fat and skin from the meat and carefully broil until bubbling and crisp.) Meanwhile, using a slotted spoon, remove the vegetables to a warm dish, reserving the liquid. Cover and keep warm.

Remove the pork from the oven, transfer to a board, loosely cover with foil, and let rest. Put the vegetable roasting pan on the stovetop, pour in a splash of hard cider, and stir over the heat. Add more stock if you don't have enough liquid in your pan with the honey, soy sauce, and a spoonful of applesauce, if using. Season and simmer for 10 minutes, then pour in any remaining pork juices and strain into a pitcher. Serve the pork with the roasted vegetables, cabbage, mashed potatoes, gravy, applesauce, and plenty of cracklings!

prepare-ahead main courses

beef wellington

splash of olive oil

2-pound piece beef tenderloin, taken from the center, with an even thickness of about 4 inches

9 ounces crimini mushrooms, very finely chopped

1 large garlic clove, finely chopped

1 tablespoon Madeira

1 (18-ounce) package refrigerated all-butter puff pastry in a block

all-purpose flour, for dusting

6 slices prosciutto

$^1/_2$ teaspoon English mustard powder

1 egg, beaten, for brushing

To serve

Madeira Sauce (see page 24)

buttered new potatoes

green beans or a green salad

The ideal main course for a special occasion—it looks as though you've been toiling all day when in fact you've been having your hair and nails done! Serve it with the Madeira Sauce on page 24.

Serves 4 to 6

Season the beef all over with black pepper. In a very hot heavy-bottom skillet, heat the oil until smoking. Add the beef and quickly brown it all over, about 5 to 10 seconds on each side, not forgetting the ends. Remove to a board and let cool completely.

Add the mushrooms to the pan and sauté over medium heat for about 5 minutes, letting them brown, but stirring occasionally. Add the garlic, stir for a minute, then add the Madeira and some salt and pepper and cook until all the liquid has evaporated. Remove to a bowl and let cool.

Take the pastry out of the fridge and roll out on a floured counter until about $^1/_8$ inch thick. Cut to fit your piece of beef (I haven't given exact measurements as tenderloins can vary so enormously in size, but the pastry will need to be large enough to wrap up your beef, with a generous overlap). Lay 4 prosciutto slices side by side on the pastry so they are touching, then spoon most of the mushroom mix over the ham and pat down. Sprinkle the beef with the mustard powder and rub all over, then place the fillet on top of the mushrooms in the center of the pastry. Spoon over the remaining mushroom mix, pat down, and lay the two final slices of prosciutto lengthwise along the beef. Carefully and tightly bring the lower pieces of prosciutto up and over the beef to wrap it. Then trim the pastry, brush all the pastry edges with beaten egg, and fold up to enclose the beef in the most dainty but efficient way you can. Place on a baking sheet lined with wax paper, with the pastry folds on the underside, and brush all over with beaten egg.

(F) Open freeze the beef on the lined baking sheet. When frozen, carefully transfer into a bag and freeze until required.

(D) Let stand for about 24 hours in the fridge before cooking.

(R) When ready to cook the beef, preheat the oven to 425°F. Remove the beef from the fridge and place on a baking sheet. Leave for 20 minutes at room temperature, then bake in the oven for 30 to 35 minutes, or until the pastry is golden brown. Let rest for 5 to 10 minutes before slicing thickly and serving with Madeira Sauce (see page 24), buttered new potatoes, and green beans or a green salad.

lamb and prune tagine

1 teaspoon coriander seeds

1 teaspoon cumin seeds

$^1/_2$ teaspoon hot paprika

$^1/_2$ teaspoon ground cinnamon

2 tablespoons olive oil

2 onions, cut into wedges

$1^3/_4$ pounds boned lamb neck slices, cut into chunks

4 garlic cloves, crushed

$1^1/_4$ cups lamb stock

1 (14-ounce) can tomatoes

$10^1/_2$ ounces sweet potatoes, peeled and cut into chunks

12 plumped pitted prunes

2 teaspoons honey

pinch of saffron threads, soaked in 1 tablespoon hot water (optional)

To serve

herby couscous

I do like the combination of fruit, meat, and spices with lots of lovely juice and buttery, herby couscous. This is a stew-like tagine using a cheap cut of meat. It's a favorite in our household—my baby has a mashed-up version!

Serves 4

Using a mortar and pestle, crush the coriander and cumin seed. Place in a bowl and stir in the paprika, cinnamon, and half the oil. Add the lamb and stir until thoroughly coated in the spice mix.

In a flameproof casserole dish or heavy-bottom pan, heat the remaining tablespoon oil over medium heat and sauté the onions until just beginning to soften and brown. Add the lamb, increase the heat, and brown all over. Add the garlic and cook, stirring, for an additional 2 minutes, then pour in the stock and tomatoes. Season, cover, and gently simmer for an hour.

Add the potatoes, prunes, honey, and saffron (if using) to the casserole and cook for an additional 45 minutes, or until the lamb is tender.

(F) Pour into a container, cool, cover, label, and freeze.

(D) Let stand overnight in the fridge.

(R) Place the tagine in a pan, bring to a boil, then let simmer gently for 15 minutes, or until piping hot. Serve with herby couscous.

fennel, leek, and potato gratin

4 tablespoons butter

2 fennel bulbs, trimmed and sliced

2 large leeks, trimmed and sliced

$2^1/_4$ pounds potatoes, peeled and cut into $^3/_8$-inch slices

2 garlic cloves, crushed

$1^1/_4$ cups heavy cream

$^2/_3$ cup milk

$1^1/_2$ cups crumbled blue cheese, such as Stilton

Great for vegetarians, but also a cheery accompaniment to leftover cold roast meat. It's a real winner on the day after Christmas!

Serves 6

In a large pan, melt the butter over gentle heat, then add the fennel and leeks and sauté, stirring, for 3 to 4 minutes. Add the potato and garlic and stir over the heat for an additional 3 minutes, then pour in the cream and milk and season with pepper. Bring to a simmer, then cook over very gentle heat, stirring occasionally, until the potatoes feel about half cooked, about 20 to 25 minutes. Stir in half the crumbled blue cheese, then transfer to a large baking dish. Sprinkle over the remaining cheese.

(**F**) Cool, then cover with foil, label, and freeze.

(**R**) Cook from frozen. Preheat the oven to 300°F. Place the foil-covered baking dish in the oven and bake for 1–$1^1/_2$ hours, or until soft when poked with a knife and bubbling.

chicken with chorizo, bell peppers, and olives

2 tablespoons olive oil

8 ounces cooked chorizo sausage, casing removed, chopped

$2^1/_4$ pounds skinless and boneless chicken thighs or breasts, cut into bite-size pieces

$^1/_2$ teaspoon sweet paprika

splash of white wine

$5^1/_2$ ounces drained roasted red bell peppers, cut into strips

$^1/_2$ batch (3–$3^1/_3$ cups) All-purpose Tomato Sauce (see page 33)

2 rosemary sprigs

about 3 tablespoons pitted black olives

A quick-fix meal or one to freeze for when friends come over.

Serves 6 to 8

In a large deep skillet, heat the oil and pan-fry the chorizo until beginning to brown and release its oil. Remove to a plate. Add the chicken to the pan and brown over high heat (you may need to do this in two batches). Return the chorizo to the pan with all the chicken and stir in the paprika. Add the wine and simmer for 2 minutes, then stir in the bell peppers, tomato sauce, and rosemary and season to taste. Simmer until the chicken is just cooked through, about 15 minutes, then stir in the olives.

(**F**) Pour the chicken into containers, then cool, cover, label, and freeze.

(**D**) Let stand overnight in the fridge.

(**R**) Place in a saucepan over low heat, stirring occasionally, until piping hot.

chicken, taleggio, and spinach crêpes

For the sauce

6 tablespoons all-purpose flour

4 tablespoons butter

2 cups plus 1 tablespoon milk

7 ounces Taleggio cheese, chopped into $^1/_2$–$^3/_4$-inch pieces

For the filling

about 1 tablespoon butter

splash of oil

1 small onion, chopped

$1^3/_4$ pounds skinless and boneless chicken thighs, cut into small chunks

2 garlic cloves, crushed

12 ounces mushrooms, cut into thickish slices

2 good pinches oregano

splash white wine

7 ounces frozen whole leaf spinach cubes, cooked and drained

$^2/_3$ cup chicken stock

8 cooked plain Crêpes (see page 30)

If you can't find Taleggio cheese, use cheddar or Gruyère instead. You can also use fresh cooked and drained spinach if you prefer. Make a double batch of the Crêpe batter (see page 30) and freeze what you don't need—either the batter or the cooked crêpes—for later.

Makes 8 crêpes (serves 4)

To make the sauce, in a saucepan, place the flour, butter, and milk and beat over medium heat until thickened. Remove the pan from the heat and add half the Taleggio and a grinding of black pepper. Stir with a wooden spoon until melted, then set aside.

To make the filling, in a large pan, heat the butter and oil and gently sauté the onion until softened, about 5 minutes. Add the chicken and cook, stirring with the onion, until sealed. Add the garlic, mushrooms, and oregano and cook for an additional 2 minutes, then pour in the wine. Bubble for a minute or so, then add about half the cheese sauce, the spinach, and the stock. Season and simmer for 2 minutes, then let cool completely.

Divide the filling among the crêpes and roll up. Place the filled crêpes in a dish and top with the remaining cheese sauce, then scatter over the remaining Taleggio.

(F) Cover with plastic wrap and foil, label, and freeze.

(D) Let stand overnight in the fridge.

(R) Preheat the oven to 350°F. Cover the dish with foil and bake for 40 to 50 minutes, or until piping hot, then brown under a hot broiler.

chicken, ham, and tarragon pie

1 (18-ounce) package refrigerated all-
   butter puff pastry in a block
all-purpose flour, for dusting
2 thick slices good-quality fully cooked
   ham, cut into strips
1 heaping tablespoon finely chopped
   fresh tarragon
$^1/_2$ quantity of Chicken with White
   Wine and Herbs (see page 35)
1 egg, beaten

The ultimate comfort food, bursting with flavorsome vegetables and a rich herby gravy. You can either use some of the pre-frozen chicken filling (see page 35), in which case thaw it, then assemble the pie and eat right away. Alternatively, you can make the filling, let cool, and assemble the pie, then freeze the whole thing uncooked ready to defrost and bake in the oven at a later date.

Serves 4

Roll out the pastry on a floured counter and, using your pie dish as a template, cut out a piece to generously fit the top. From the trimmings, cut a $^3/_4$-inch wide strip (it can be in pieces) to fit around the rim of the dish. Dampen the edges and stick the strips in place around the rim.

Mix the ham and tarragon into the chicken filling, then spoon this into the dish. Dampen the top of the pastry strip and place the pastry round on top. Trim the edges and press down gently. Decorate the top if you wish with pastry shapes made from the trimmings, then brush with the beaten egg and make a small slit in the top for a steam hole. Either freeze or cook within 4 hours (keep the pie in the fridge).

(F) Cover the pie dish, label, and freeze.

(D) Let stand overnight in the fridge.

(C) Remove the pie from the fridge 20 minutes before cooking. Preheat the oven to 375°F. Bake the pie for 30 to 35 minutes, or until piping hot and deep golden.

crab cakes with citrus and avocado salad

1 pound potatoes, peeled and cut
   into large chunks
$5^{1}/_{2}$ ounces skinless cod fillet
$^{2}/_{3}$ cup whole milk
2 tablespoons butter
4 scallions, trimmed and chopped
1 large garlic clove
1 heaping tablespoon all-purpose flour
zest of 1 and juice $^{1}/_{2}$ lime
2 pinches cayenne pepper
2 (6-ounce) cans lump white
   crabmeat, drained, or 9 ounces fresh
   lump white crabmeat
2 tablespoons chopped fresh cilantro
5 to 6 tablespoons semolina
vegetable oil, for frying

For the citrus salad

1 avocado, peeled, pitted, and sliced
1 orange, segmented
1 pink grapefruit, segmented
2 to 3 handfuls herb salad
1 to 2 tablespoons olive oil

I like the addition of a small amount of fish in these, purely because they add a little more texture and the poaching liquid gives the mixture a bit more depth of flavor. Use fresh crabmeat if you can get it.

Makes 12 small crab cakes (3 each or 2 for an appetizer)

In a saucepan, boil the potatoes in salted water until soft, then drain. Meanwhile, in a separate pan, bring the fish to a simmer in the milk, then simmer until cooked through, about 5 minutes. Remove from the milk to a plate (reserving the milk). In another saucepan, melt the butter and sauté the scallions and garlic for 2 minutes. Stir in the flour, then gradually incorporate the poaching milk and bring to a boil. Simmer for 2 minutes. Add the potato and, using a potato masher, mash until smooth. Flake in the fish, then stir in the lime zest and juice. Season with a sprinkle of salt, cayenne, and ground black pepper and extra lime juice, to taste. When cool, stir in the crabmeat and cilantro, then let stand in the fridge for about an hour to cool completely. Sprinkle half the semolina onto a board. With wet hands, shape the cold fish mixture into 12 cakes and sit on the semolina. Sprinkle over the remaining semolina to coat and carefully transfer to a board or tray covered in wax paper.

(F) Open freeze the cakes, then bag and label.

(C) Pan-fry the cakes from frozen gently in the oil for 6 to 8 minutes each side until golden and piping hot. Mix the salad greens with the avocado, orange, grapefruit, a drizzle of olive oil, and some seasoning. Serve with the crab cakes.

eggplant and lentil moussaka

My stepmother, Wendy, is a fabulous cook, who has the knack of producing incredible food, from wherever, using whatever, in what seems like minutes! She made the tastiest moussaka for us on a wonderful holiday for my father's 60th birthday in Greece a few years ago. This is a veggie version!

Serves 4 to 6

5 tablespoons olive oil

1 medium eggplant, trimmed and cut into $^1/_2$-inch slices

14 ounces potatoes, peeled and cut into $^1/_2$-inch slices

$^2/_3$ cup shredded cheddar

For the vegetable and lentil sauce

1 medium onion, chopped

1 medim zucchini, trimmed and chopped

1 red bell pepper, seeded and chopped

2 garlic cloves, crushed

$^1/_2$ teaspoon ground cinnamon

$1^1/_2$ tablespoons tomato paste

splash of red wine (optional)

1 (24–26-ounce) jar or pack strained tomatoes with garlic and herbs

1 (14-ounce) can green lentils, rinsed and drained

1 to 2 pinches white sugar

For the ricotta sauce

6 tablespoons all-purpose flour

4 tablespoons butter

$1^1/_4$ cups milk

good grating of nutmeg

1 cup ricotta cheese

In a skillet, heat a tablespoon of the oil and pan-fry the eggplant slices in batches, on both sides, until browned and beginning to soften. Transfer to a plate lined with paper towels while you cook the rest. (Add a little more oil if necessary to prevent from sticking, but wait until it is very hot before adding the eggplant slices or they will be soggy and oily.) Set to one side.

Meanwhile, make the sauce. In a clean pan, heat a tablespoon of the oil and sauté the onion for 2 minutes. Add the chopped zucchini and bell pepper and gently sauté for about 5 minutes, then add the garlic and cook until the vegetables begin to soften, about 2 minutes more. Stir in the cinnamon and tomato paste and cook for about a minute before adding the red wine, if using, and after an additional minute the strained tomatoes. Simmer for 10 minutes, then stir in the lentils, sugar, and seasoning.

Meanwhile, in a saucepan, boil the potato slices in salted water until half cooked, about 3 minutes. Drain and let cool slightly while you make the ricotta sauce. In a saucepan, place the flour, butter, and milk and beat over medium heat. When thickened, season with salt, pepper, and some grated nutmeg and let cool for 5 minutes, then beat in the ricotta.

Pour half the vegetable sauce into the bottom of a deep round casserole or baking dish with about a 3-quart capacity. Top with the potato slices in one layer, then spread over half the ricotta sauce. Layer on half the eggplant, followed by the remaining vegetable sauce, the rest of the eggplant, and then the last of the ricotta sauce. Top with the shredded cheddar.

(**F**) Cool. Cover with foil or a lid, label, and freeze.

(**D**) Let stand for at least 24 hours in the fridge. Remove and thaw at room temperature if necessary.

(**C**) Preheat the oven to 375°F. Bake for 45 to 55 minutes, or until piping hot and bubbling.

slow-roast leg of lamb

For the roast lamb

2 ($3^3/4$-pound) frozen leg of lamb

3 tablespoons olive oil

6 large carrots, peeled and cut into
2-inch lengths

4 celery stalks, trimmed and cut into
2-inch lengths

2 large onions, halved

2 garlic heads, halved widthwise

2 anchovy fillets

3 rosemary sprigs

3 bay leaves

2 tablespoons tomato paste

$3^1/3$ cups chicken stock

2 cups white wine

For the gravy

1 heaping teaspoon red currant jelly

dash of soy sauce

To serve

roast potatoes or Fennel, Leek, and
Potato Gratin (see page 84)

green vegetable of your choice

Yes, you really can cook a joint from frozen! However, if you are cooking a fresh joint, simply reduce the sizzling time at the higher temperature to 25 minutes at the beginning and slow roast for 3 hours rather than 5. I have suggested using two shoulders, to make life easier and save on energy: you can roast both, eat one right away with a gratin, such as the one on page 84, and turn the second into the Smart Shepherd's Pie (see opposite) that you can store in the freezer for a later occasion—or even turn both into pies. Of course, if you prefer, you can just halve the recipe.

Serves 4 to 6

Take the lamb from the freezer an hour before cooking and place in a large roasting pan. Preheat the oven to 425°F.

Drizzle the lamb with the oil and season with salt and pepper. Roast for 35 minutes, then reduce the heat to 300°F. Remove the lamb from the oven, lift the meat up, and scatter the carrot, celery, onion, garlic, anchovies, rosemary, and bay leaves underneath. Mix the tomato paste into the hot stock, then pour over the lamb along with the wine. Cover fairly tightly with a layer of foil and bake for 5 hours.

Remove the lamb from the oven, and transfer one to a separate dish along with half the vegetables, garlic, and juices. Let cool before chilling until completely cold.

For the roast, pour the remaining lamb juices into a small saucepan, carefully skimming off some of the fat from the top as you do so. Squeeze out half a head of the garlic into the pan. Add the red currant jelly and soy sauce and simmer for a few minutes. Strain and serve with the carved lamb, roast potatoes or the Fennel, Leek, and Potato Gratin on page 84, the remaining carrots and onions from the roasting pan, and a green vegetable.

smart shepherd's pie

$1/2$ quantity Slow-roast Lamb
   Shoulder (see opposite), cooled
$2^1/4$ pounds potatoes, peeled
$3/4$ cup plus 1 tablespoon milk
3 tablespoons butter
good grating of nutmeg

Using the lamb shoulder roast (opposite) turns this recipe from everyday to special occasion. For even more variety, try using a mix of potato and celery root in the mash, too. The Ground Beef For All Occasions (page 34) is another filling you can use with this topping—just thaw and follow the same cooking instructions.

Serves 4 to 6

Remove as much of the surface fat as you can from the lamb shoulder, then transfer the lamb and vegetables to a dish and the juices to a pitcher.

In a large saucepan, boil the potatoes until tender and then strain. In a small saucepan, heat the milk and butter, then add to the potatoes before mashing. Season with salt, pepper, and nutmeg and let cool completely.

Take all the meat off the bone and cut into bite-size pieces, discarding any lumps of fat. Cut the vegetables into smaller chunks and squeeze out the garlic cloves into the juices. Top up the juices to $1^2/3$ cups with a little water or stock if necessary. Put the meat and vegetables into a baking dish and pour over the gravy. Top with the mash.

(F) Cover the dish, label, and freeze.

(D) Let stand overnight in the fridge.

(C) Preheat the oven to 350°F. Cook for 40 to 50 minutes, or until golden and bubbling.

smoked fish, crab, and watercress tart

$^1/_2$ quantity Pie Dough (see page 28) or 1 (14-ounce) box refrigerated ready-rolled pie crust

8 ounces fresh smoked cod or salmon fillet, flaked

$1^2/_3$ cups whole milk

2 eggs, beaten

about 1 tablespoon butter

1 medium leek, trimmed and chopped

2 tablespoons all-purpose flour

1 to 2 pinches cayenne pepper

$3^1/_2$ ounces fresh white lump crabmeat

$3^1/_2$ ounces fresh brown crabmeat

$1^3/_4$ ounces trimmed watercress, chopped

I adore the combination of smoked fish and watercress, and the addition of some fresh crab makes this a perfect summer entertaining recipe.

Serves 6 to 8

You will need a round loose-bottom tart pan $9^1/_2$ inches in diameter and 1-inch deep and some dried beans.

Preheat the oven to 375°F. If using the block of dough, on a floured counter, roll the dough out to a large circle. Line the tart pan with the rolled-out dough or ready-rolled sheet and chill for 30 minutes. Scrunch up some wax paper, place in the tart shell, and fill with dried beans. Bake in the oven for 15 minutes.

In a baking dish, place the fish and milk, cover with foil, and poach in the oven for 20 minutes. Remove the foil and transfer the fish to a dish to cool, then flake. Reserve the poaching milk.

Remove the paper and beans from the tart and brush with a little of the beaten egg. Return the tart shell to the oven for an additional 5 minutes.

In a saucepan, melt the butter and sauté the leek gently until softened. Add the flour and stir. Gradually stir in the poaching milk and bring to a boil. Season with cayenne, salt, and pepper. Simmer for 2 to 3 minutes, then place the pan in a sink a quarter full of cold water to help cool. When the sauce is completely cold, add the crabmeat, flaked smoked fish, watercress, and beaten eggs and stir carefully before pouring it into the tart shell.

(**F**) Cover the uncooked tart, still in its pan, with plastic wrap, then freeze. When frozen, carefully remove from the pan and transfer to a bag.

(**D**) When ready to cook, place the tart back in the pan and thaw overnight in the fridge.

(**C**) Preheat the oven to 350°F. Place a cookie sheet in the oven to heat (heating the sheet will ensure the crust isn't soggy). Place the tart on the hot baking sheet and bake for 30 to 40 minutes until just set and golden. Let rest for a few minutes before serving.

aromatic lamb curry

2 good splashes vegetable oil
2-inch piece cinnamon stick
12 cloves
12 cardamon pods
3 teaspoons cumin seed
3 onions, finely diced
12 garlic cloves, crushed
$2^3/_4$-inch piece fresh ginger, peeled and
  finely grated
2 (14-ounce) cans diced tomatoes
3 green chiles, slit (seeded
  if you prefer a less fiery curry)
$^3/_4$ teaspoon hot chili powder
1 heaping teaspoon flaked sea salt
$3^1/_4$ pounds boneless lamb, cut into
  chunks

To serve
large handful of chopped fresh cilantro
dhal or rice
naan
steamed green beans tossed with
  butter and black onion seed

Curry Queen Sheila Damodaran gave me her recipe for a quick-to-prepare lamb curry to include in this book, as she is passionate about cooking healthy Indian food for families. This works best with diced lamb shoulder but would be fine with diced leg, too. As it is a reasonably dry curry, serve it with dhal and naan.

Serves 4

In a heavy-bottom saucepan, heat the oil and add the whole spices. When they begin to sizzle, add the onions and sauté until golden brown in color, about 8 minutes. Add the garlic and ginger and cook for an additional 1 to 2 minutes.

Add the tomatoes, whole chiles, chili powder, and salt and cook until the sauce is thick, about 10 to 12 minutes.

Add the meat and bring to a boil, then pour in $^3/_4$ cup boiling water and reduce the heat until barely simmering. (The secret of a very tender meat curry is never to let it boil vigorously.) Cook for $1^3/_4$–2 hours, or until very tender, with the lid resting on the top. Check occasionally that the curry is not becoming too dry and add a little extra water if necessary.

(F) Cool, then pour into freezer containers, label, and freeze.

(D) Let stand overnight in the fridge.

(R) Place the curry in a pan, bring to a boil, and then simmer gently for 15 minutes, or until piping hot. Add the cilantro and serve with some dhal or rice, naan, and some steamed green beans tossed with butter and black onion seed.

beef and spinach lasagna

4 tablespoons butter
6 tablespoons all-purpose flour
$1^{3}/_{4}$ cups plus 2 tablespoons milk
$10^{1}/_{2}$ ounces frozen leaf spinach cubes
$^{2}/_{3}$ cup shredded sharp cheddar cheese
$^{1}/_{2}$ cup grated Parmesan cheese
grated nutmeg
$^{1}/_{4}$ batch Ground Beef For All
   Occasions (see page 34)
6 to 8 dry lasagna noodles

Lasagna is a favorite with most families and this version uses the Ground Meat For All Occasions on page 34. Either make the lasagna using freshly made and cooled ground beef (before it has been frozen) and freeze the prepared dish uncooked, or thaw a container of the Ground Meat For All Occasions, prepare the lasagna, and cook it straight away. If you are cooking for larger numbers, just double the quantities and prepare in a larger dish. It may need an extra 10 minutes in the oven just to ensure the center gets piping hot. You can use fresh spinach if you prefer—just stir the cooked and drained spinach into the hot white sauce.

Serves 4

First make the sauce. In a saucepan, melt the butter over low heat, stir in the flour, and cook for 2 minutes. Gradually incorporate the milk and bring to a boil. Stir in the frozen spinach cubes and simmer until thawed. Remove the pan from the heat, mix the cheeses together, and add half to the sauce. Stir until the cheese has melted and season with grated nutmeg and salt and pepper. Let cool.

When the sauce is cool, assemble the lasagna. Put half the ground beef in the base of a 2-quart baking dish, top with about 3 lasagna noodles, then spread over just under half the spinach sauce. Lay another 3 lasagna noodles over the top, then spoon over the remainder of the meat sauce and finish with the remainder of the spinach sauce. Scatter over the remaining cheese. Either cook (if using thawed ground beef) or freeze (if using freshly made ground beef) at this point.

(D) Let stand overnight in the fridge.

(C) Preheat the oven to 350°F. Cook the lasagna for 35 to 45 minutes, or until golden, bubbling, and piping hot.

ox cheeks with red wine and mushrooms

Don't let the cut of meat put you off—once you have tried these, I'm sure you will love them. However it is also delicious made with chuck steak.

1 (1-ounce) package mixed dried
mushrooms (I used porcini, oyster,
and shiitake)
3 heaping tablespoons all-purpose
flour
$3^3/_4$ pounds ox (beef) cheeks, cut in
half, or chuck steak, cut into
large chunks
2 to 3 tablespoons vegetable oil
4 thick slices smoked bacon, chopped
2 red onions, cut into wedges
2 celery stalks, trimmed and sliced
2 garlic cloves, crushed
$1^1/_2$ tablespoons tomato paste
2 tablespoons red currant jelly
$1^2/_3$ cups full-bodied red wine
2 bay leaves
1 rosemary sprig
1 (14-ounce) can beef consommé or
$1^2/_3$ cups beef stock if you have it

To serve
about 1 tablespoon butter
6 large portobello mushrooms, sliced
2 tablespoons chopped fresh parsley
creamy celery root and potato mash or
dauphinoise potatoes
green leafy vegetable

Serves 6 to 8

Soak the dried mushrooms in a measuring cup with $^3/_4$ cup hot water for 30 minutes. Preheat the oven to 300°F. Season the flour with plenty of salt and pepper, then toss the ox cheeks or chuck steak in the flour until coated.

In a large, heavy-bottom skillet, heat 1 tablespoon of the oil, add the bacon, and cook until just crisp. Transfer to a plate and set aside.

Add a little more oil to the pan and heat until smoking. Add about half the floured meat (you don't want the pan to be crowded) and cook for about 3 minutes until really brown, pushing down on the pieces with a spatula to help them brown faster. Turn over and brown the other sides and edges. Transfer to a casserole dish, then cook the remaining meat in the same way, adding a little extra oil if needed.

Once you have added the last of the meat to the casserole dish, turn the heat down under the skillet, add the onions and celery, and soften gently for about 10 minutes. Squeeze the liquid from the soaked dried mushrooms into a bowl and reserve, then add the mushrooms and garlic to the onions and celery. Cook for an additional 2 minutes, then increase the heat, stir in the tomato paste, red currant jelly, and red wine, and bubble for 3 minutes. Add to the casserole dish with the bacon, herbs, and consommé or beef stock and mushroom soaking liquid. Cover and cook in the oven for 3 hours.

(F) Using a slotted spoon, remove the meat and vegetables to a container. Taste and season the sauce, adding salt, pepper, or red currant jelly if needed, then pour over the meat. Cool, cover with a lid, label, and freeze.

(D) Let stand for at least 24 hours in the fridge.

(R) Preheat the oven to 350°F. In a skillet, melt the butter and sauté the mushrooms for 3 to 4 minutes. Return the meat, vegetables, and sauce to a flameproof casserole dish. Add the mushrooms, bring to a simmer, cover, and place in the oven for 25 minutes. Reduce the heat to 300°F and cook for 45 minutes. Sprinkle with parsley and serve with mash or dauphinoise potatoes and greens.

baked treats

quick double-chocolate sheet cake

$^3/_4$ cup plus $2^1/_2$ tablespoons butter, softened

1 cup superfine sugar

4 large eggs

$^1/_4$ cup unsweetened cocoa, dissolved in 3 to 4 tablespoons boiling water to make a smooth paste

$1^2/_3$ cups less 1 tablespoon self-rising flour

$^1/_2$ teaspoon baking powder

$3^1/_2$ ounces semisweet chocolate chips

chocolate buttons, M&Ms, or fresh raspberries, to decorate

For the frosting

1 tablespoon unsweetened cocoa, dissolved in 2 tablespoons boiling water to make a paste

$5^1/_2$ tablespoons butter, softened

$1^2/_3$ cups confectioners' sugar

Pooh, my mother-in-law, makes the best easy family-style chocolate cake, which we persuade her to make whenever there's a birthday! Her secret is dissolving the cocoa in boiling water before adding it. If you prefer, you can divide this among two round cake pans and add a filling layer.

Makes 12 to 14 pieces

Preheat the oven to 350°F. Grease and line a 11 x 7 x 2-inch baking pan.

In a large bowl, place the softened butter, sugar, eggs, and dissolved cocoa. Sift over the flour and baking powder. Using a hand mixer, beat the mixture until it is pale and creamy, about 2 minutes. Using a metal spoon, fold in the chocolate chips.

Turn the mixture into the greased pan and spread it out evenly. Bake for 30 to 35 minutes, or until risen and springy to the touch. Cool slightly before turning out onto a wire rack.

Once the cake is cool, in a bowl, place all the frosting ingredients and, using the hand mixer, beat together well. Spread over the cake. Run a fork across the surface of the frosting to create a wavy pattern of lines.

(**F**) Place the frosted cake on a tray or plate and open freeze. Once frozen, place in a box or freezer bag and return to the freezer.

(**D**) Let stand overnight on a wire rack, then sprinkle with your topping of choice.

freezer cookies

3 cups all-purpose flour
1 heaping teaspoon baking powder
$^3/_4$ cup superfine sugar
1 cup plus 2 tablespoons butter,
  softened
1 large egg, beaten
1 teaspoon vanilla extract

For the decoration (optional)
confectioners' sugar
lemon juice (or water)
food coloring and/or edible
  decorations

These are just what freezer cookies should be: versatile, melt in the mouth, and child-proof—they can roll out the dough countless times and it will still taste good! I've given some flavor variations but you can devise others— the possibilities are endless! I tend to use some of the mixture right away, then freeze the rest for later. My friend Anna inspired me to include these as she has a great Scandinavian recipe for lemon cookies, which she often makes with her son Sasha—a great activity for a rainy day!

Makes about 40 cookies

Sift the flour, baking powder, and a pinch of salt together into a bowl. In another bowl, place the butter and sugar and beat using a hand mixer until combined. Add the dry ingredients, egg, and vanilla extract and beat again. Using floured hands, form the mixture into a ball. If cooking and eating right away, follow the directions below to roll the mixture into 2 sausage shapes and slice into $^1/_2$-inch thick slices. Bake as directed below. Alternatively, choose one of the following three options:

Freeze, slice, and bake

Divide the mixture into 2 equal portions and, using your hands, roll each out on a floured counter to form a sausage shape measuring about $1^1/_2$–2 inches in diameter. Wrap each sausage in plastic wrap and freeze. When you are ready to bake the cookies, remove from the freezer about 15 minutes before, then slice into 1/2-inch thick slices and bake as directed below.

Cut into shapes, freeze, and then bake

Form the dough into a ball, wrap in plastic wrap, and chill for 20 minutes. Roll out on a floured counter to about $^1/_2$ inch thick, use cookie cutters to cut into shapes, and freeze the uncooked cookies between sheets of wax paper. Bake from frozen as needed.

Cut into shapes, bake, and then freeze

Cut out shapes as above, bake, and then freeze the baked cookies and thaw on a wire rack as needed.

(C) Preheat the oven to 350°F. Place a sheet of parchment paper on a cookie sheet, then space the cookies $1^1/_2$–2 inches apart on the paper. Bake for 12 to 18 minutes, depending on whether or not you are cooking them from frozen (they should be just starting to take on color around the edges when ready). Transfer to a wire rack and let cool completely.

To frost: If you like you can frost the cookies. Just mix some confectioners' sugar with a few drops of water or lemon juice and blend until smooth and just pourable (mix in a little food coloring at this point if you like). Drizzle or spread the frosting over the cookies, once cooled, and top with sprinkles or other edible decorations as you wish.

Variations:

Each of the following variations uses a half quantity of freezer cookie dough. You can split the dough into 2 equal portions in 2 separate bowls and use a wooden spoon to mix in the additional ingredients.

Pistachio—Mix in 2 tablespoons of shelled, chopped pistachios. Form into a sausage or roll out as per recipe opposite. Alternatively, simply press the chopped nuts into the side of plain cookies before baking.

Chocolate orange—Mix in 1 tablespoon of sifted unsweetened cocoa and the zest of 1 large orange. (This gives a subtle orange flavor—add more zest for a stronger orange taste.) Form into a sausage or roll out as per recipe opposite.

Oat and sultana—Mix scant $^2/_3$ cup rolled oats and 2 heaping tablespoons golden raisins. Form into a sausage or roll out as per recipe opposite.

Honey and almond—Replace 2 tablespoons of the sugar with 2 teaspoons well-flavored honey and add 2 tablespoons toasted slivered almonds. Form into a sausage or roll out as per recipe opposite.

healthier granola bars

$^2/_3$ cup butter

$^1/_2$ cup raw brown sugar

scant $^1/_3$ cup golden syrup or
   dark corn syrup

3 cups rolled oats

$3^1/_2$ ounces dried mixed berries

1 apple, peeled, cored, and shredded

$1^1/_2$ tablespoons sesame seeds

I often put a frozen bar in my son William's lunchbox and it is always thawed in time for his lunch. These are a healthier alternative to normal granola bars, but without the taste and texture of cardboard! Personally, I don't really see the point in making occasional treats if they are so packed with "healthy" things that they no longer taste nice!

Makes 15 bars

Preheat the oven to 350°F. Grease a $8^1/_2$ x 7-inch baking pan and line it with wax paper. (I always leave some paper hanging over the edges of the pan, as it acts as a good handle when lifting out the cooled slab.)

In a saucepan, heat the butter, sugar, and syrup gently until the butter has melted and the sugar is beginning to dissolve.

In a bowl, place the oats, dried mixed berries, apple, and sesame seed into and stir together, then pour over the hot butter, sugar, and syrup mixture and mix thoroughly. Turn the mixture into the greased and lined pan and bake for 20 to 25 minutes.

Let cool for 10 minutes before cutting into 15 bars in the pan. When cold, remove the slab from the pan and layer the bars between sheets of wax paper in a plastic container.

(**F**) Cover the container, then label and freeze.

(**D**) Let stand at room temperature for 2 to 3 hours.

buttercream sponge

1 cup very soft butter

1 cup plus 2 tablespoons superfine sugar

4 large eggs, beaten

2 teaspoons baking powder

4 tablespoons orange juice or milk

$1^3/_4$ cups plus 1 tablespoon self-rising flour

For the filling

7 tablespoons soft butter

$^1/_3$ cup cream cheese

$1^1/_2$ cups confectioners' sugar, plus extra for dusting

1 teaspoon vanilla extract

4 to 5 tablespoons soft-set raspberry or strawberry jam

I was taught how to cook at school by Mrs. Wilkinson and Mrs. Jackson. I can still hear the latter shouting out in her Yorkshire accent "don't forget to greeeeze your baking sheets." I was taught that the simplest way to remember to make a sponge is to remember it is the same number in ounces (in this case 8 ounces) of butter, sugar, and flour with half the quantity of eggs (4 eggs)—an easy rule for children to remember, too. I've added cream cheese to the filling to make it fresher tasting, but you can make regular buttercream or use thick cream if you prefer.

Serves 8 to 10

Preheat the oven to 375°F. Grease a loose-bottom cake pan 8 inches in diameter and $3^1/_2$ inches deep.

If you want to save time, you can put all the sponge ingredients into a stand mixer, sifting over the flour and baking powder last. Mix for about 2 minutes until well combined, turn it into the pan, and bake.

Alternatively (which I think gives the better result), in a large bowl, place the soft butter and sugar. Using a hand mixer, or wooden spoon if you have good arm muscles, beat until the batter is light, pale, and creamy, about 2 minutes. Add the egg, bit by bit, beating well, adding a tablespoon of the flour toward the end to stop it splitting.

Remove the mixer and sift over the flour and baking powder. Using a large metal spoon, fold lightly until combined, adding the orange juice or milk toward the end. Pour into the cake pan and lightly spread out. Place in the center of the oven and bake for 40 to 45 minutes, or until springy to the touch and a skewer comes out clean when inserted. Let cool slightly, then remove to a wire rack to cool completely.

Meanwhile, beat the butter, cream cheese, sugar, and vanilla until combined. Halve the cake horizontally across the center and spread the base with the filling. Lightly spread over the jam and top with the second cake.

(F) Open freeze, then carefully put into a bag, label, and freeze.

(D) Let stand on a wire rack for 5 to 6 hours. Dust with confectioners' sugar before serving.

st. clement's drizzle cake

$^3/_4$ cup soft butter

1 cup superfine sugar

zest of 1 orange

zest of 1 lemon

3 large eggs

1$^1/_2$ cups plus 1 tablespoon self-rising flour, sifted

$^1/_3$ cup plus 1 tablespoon whole milk

1 teaspoon baking powder, sifted

For the syrup

$^1/_2$ cup superfine sugar

juice of 1 lemon

juice of $^1/_2$ orange

I always think of summer when I think of St. Clement's: the bright colors of orange and yellow evoke a feeling of warm sunny days. The name refers to the nursery rhyme, "Oranges and Lemons," the next line of which is, "Say the bells of St. Clement's." This cake is zingy and fresh tasting—and an easy one to throw together.

Makes 12 squares

Preheat the oven to 350°F. Grease and line a 9$^1/_2$ x 8 x 2-inch baking pan.

In a bowl, place the butter, the 1 cup sugar, and the orange and lemon zests. Using a hand mixer, beat until pale and fluffy. Beat in the eggs, one at a time, then add about half the flour and half the milk. Beat until incorporated, then add the remaining flour and milk and baking powder and beat again.

Pour the mixture into the greased and lined baking pan and spread out. Bake for 30 to 35 minutes, or until golden and springy to the touch. Remove from the oven and let cool for 5 minutes while you prepare the syrup.

Mix together the $^1/_2$ cup sugar with the lemon and orange juice. Carefully remove the cake from the pan, transferring it to a sheet of foil on a board. Pierce the top of the cake all over with a skewer, then lift up the edges of the foil to ensure no syrup escapes while you drizzle it all over the cake. Let cool completely.

(**F**) Transfer the cake on the board to the freezer. Open freeze, then remove the board and wrap in foil.

(**D**) Let stand at room temperature for 4 hours.

blueberry, almond, and orange cupcakes

$^1/_2$ cup butter, softened
$^1/_2$ cup plus 1 tablespoon superfine
   sugar
2 eggs
$^1/_2$ cup ground almonds
zest of $^1/_2$ small orange plus
   2 tablespoons juice
1 cup less 1 tablespoon self-rising flour
1 teaspoon baking powder
$^2/_3$ cup blueberries

To serve
confectioners' sugar, for dusting

I love baking with my three-year-old, William, though it tends to end up with me desperately trying to get the mixture in the pans before it's eaten! Blueberries are a favorite of his: indeed, as I write this, there's a little purple mouth smiling up at me—he has just gobbled all the remaining blueberries! They also freeze beautifully: if you get the urge to bake, you can simply take them from the freezer and thaw them for about 30 minutes while you prepare the batter.

Makes about 15

You will need 2 (12-hole) muffin pans and at least 15 paper liners.

Preheat the oven to 375°F. In a bowl, place the butter, sugar, eggs, ground almonds, and orange zest and juice. Sift over the flour and baking powder. Using a hand mixer, beat until smooth and fluffy, about 2 minutes. Fold in the blueberries and then spoon the batter evenly into the liners. Bake for 15 to 20 minutes.

(F) Let cool on a wire rack, then open freeze, pack into bags, and label.

(D) Thaw them on a wire rack to prevent them from going soggy. Dust with confectioners' sugar before serving.

golden raisin scones

1³/₄ cups plus 1 tablespoon self-rising
  flour
1¹/₂ heaping teaspoons baking powder
pinch salt
4 tablespoons butter, chilled, diced
2 tablespoons white sugar
3 tablespoons golden raisins
7 to 8 tablespoons whole milk
2 teaspoons lemon juice
1 large egg, beaten

Scones freeze very well and are a lovely occasional treat to have to hand. I love golden raisin scones warmed through and buttered, but you can go all out and serve them with cream and jam if you feel like a real feast! If you don't have a cookie cutter you can cut them into squares using a knife.

Makes 6 to 8

You will need a 2¹/₂-inch fluted cookie cutter.

Preheat the oven to 425°F. Sift the flour and baking powder into a bowl and stir in the salt. Using the tips of your fingers, rub in the butter, lifting the flour to aerate it as you do so. Stir in the sugar and golden raisins.

Mix 7 tablespoons of milk with the lemon juice and egg and stir nearly all of it into the flour mixture using a table knife (you need a little drop for brushing the tops). Add a little extra milk if needed to form a stiff dough.

Turn out the dough onto a lightly floured counter and pat out gently to a square about 1¹/₄ inches thick. Use the cutter to stamp out the scones (if you dip the cutter into a little flour first, it will cut through the dough more easily). Alternatively, cut into squares using a knife. Brush the tops of the scones with the remaining egg mixture. Use an offset spatula to transfer the scones to a baking sheet lined with wax paper. Bake for 10 to 12 minutes, or until risen and golden brown. Cool on a wire rack.

(F) Place in a freezer bag, label, and freeze.

(D) Let stand at room temperature for 1 to 2 hours on a wire rack.

(R) Preheat the oven to 350°F and bake for 5 to 8 minutes.

Variation:

Blueberry scones—Replace the golden raisins with 3 tablespoons blueberries.

bacon, cheddar, and sunflower squares

4 slices smoked bacon, finely chopped

2 cups plus 1 tablespoon self-rising whole wheat or white flour, sifted

$^1/_2$ teaspoon salt

$^1/_2$ teaspoon English mustard powder

1 teaspoon baking powder

2 tablespoons butter, chilled, diced

scant 1 cup shredded cheddar

7 to 8 tablespoons whole milk

1 large egg, beaten

about 2 teaspoons sunflower seeds

These are a cross between a scone and soda bread in taste and are lovely served up next to a bowl of soup or popped into the oven for a quick snack.

Makes 9

Preheat the oven to 425°F. In a small, dry skillet, cook the bacon until crisp, then remove to a plate lined with paper towels.

In a large bowl, stir together the flour, salt, mustard powder, and baking powder, then add the butter. Using the tips of your fingers, rub in the butter, lifting the flour to aerate it as you do so. Stir in the cheddar and the bacon.

Mix 7 tablespoons of milk and the beaten egg together and pour nearly all of it into the bowl. Using a table knife, mix until combined. Add extra milk if needed to form a stiff dough.

Turn out onto a floured counter and form into a square shape about 1$^1/_4$ inches thick. Cut into 9 squares. Brush the tops of the squares with the remaining egg mixture, scatter with the sunflower seeds, and place on a baking sheet lined with wax paper. Bake for about 15 to 18 minutes, or until risen and golden.

(F) Cool on a wire rack, then place in a freezer bag, label, and freeze.

(D) Let stand for 1 to 2 hours at room temperature on a wire rack.

(R) Place in an oven preheated to 350°F for 5 to 10 minutes until warm.

choca-mocha loaf with mascarpone frosting

3/4 cup plus 2 tablespoons butter, softened
1 cup superfine sugar
4 eggs
2 teaspoons espresso coffee powder dissolved in 1 tablespoon hot water
1³/4 cups plus 1 tablespoon self-rising flour
1 teaspoon baking powder
1 tablespoon unsweetened cocoa mixed with 2 tablespoons hot water

For the frosting
1/3 cup mascarpone cheese
4 tablespoons butter
1 teaspoon espresso powder mixed with 2 teaspoons hot water
2 cups confectioners' sugar, sifted

To serve
unsweetened cocoa, for dusting
toasted walnut pieces

For those who find chocolate cake a bit too rich and coffee cake not rich enough, this choca-mocha loaf is perfect!

Serves 8

Preheat the oven to 350°F. Grease and line a 2-pound loaf pan.

In a bowl, place the butter, sugar, eggs, coffee mixture, flour, and baking powder. Using a hand mixer, beat for about 2 minutes until pale and creamy. Transfer half the mixture to a second bowl and mix in the cocoa mixture. Add tablespoonfuls of the two batters randomly to the prepared loaf pan, then level the top. Bake for 45 to 55 minutes until risen and a skewer inserted into the cake comes out clean. Let cool for about 5 minutes in the pan, then turn out onto a wire rack to cool completely.

Beat together the frosting ingredients, then spread over the top of the cooled cake. (If the mixture is a little too runny, just place in the fridge to stiffen up for 10 minutes or so.)

(F) Open freeze, then carefully place in a freezer bag.

(D) Let stand overnight, then dust with cocoa and scatter with toasted walnuts to serve.

easy mince pies

I have to admit, my family wouldn't care if I never made another mince pie again. However, I love my family tradition of making them at Christmas time, even though I'll probably be the only one eating them and end up feeling like Santa Claus at the end of his rounds!

Makes about 16

$1/2$ quantity homemade Sweet Pie
    Dough (see page 28) or
    1 (18-ounce) package all-butter
    pie dough in a block, thawed if frozen
1 (14-ounce) jar good-quality
    mincemeat
a little milk
1 egg, beaten
superfine sugar, for sprinkling

You will need 2 (12-hole) muffin pans and 3-inch and $2^1/2$-inch fluted cookie cutters.

Preheat the oven to 375°F. Roll out the pie dough on a floured counter until it is really thin (or you will end up with just crust and no filling). Using the 3-inch fluted pastry cutter, cut 16 circles (you may get a couple more, depending on how efficient you've been with your rolling), then the same again using the slightly smaller cutter.

Line the pan holes with the larger pastry circles. Spoon a heaping teaspoon of mincemeat into each pie shell and brush the dough edges with milk. Top with the smaller dough circles and press down around the edges to seal. Using the point of a knife or scissors, make two little slits in the top of each. Bake for 25 to 30 minutes, or until golden.

(**F**) Cool the mince pies in the pan, then transfer them to a container between layers of wax paper.

(**R**) Preheat the oven to 375°F. Place the frozen pies on a cookie sheet and reheat for 8 to 10 minutes.

raspberry and white chocolate muffins

3/4 cup whole milk
1 large egg
2 tablespoons vegetable oil
1/2 teaspoon vanilla extract
2 cups self-rising flour
3/4 cup superfine sugar
3 1/2 ounces white chocolate chunks
heaping 3/4 cup raspberries

To serve
confectioners' sugar, for dusting

Great to make with little ones, these muffins couldn't be simpler and are delicious eaten warm or at room temperature. Golden raisins, blueberries, semisweet chocolate, and pecans are some of the other ingredients you could add to the basic mixture—just experiment with what you fancy!

Makes 12

You will need a 12-hole muffin pan and paper liners (or use a silicone muffin pan).

Preheat the oven to 375°F. In a pitcher, combine the milk, egg, oil, and vanilla and beat. Sift the flour into a bowl and stir in the sugar, a pinch of salt, the chocolate chunks, and raspberries. Make a well in the center and pour in the liquids. Using a fork, stir gently to combine (don't overstir or the muffins won't rise).

Place the liners in the muffin pan and spoon the mixture evenly into the liners. Bake for 20 to 25 minutes, or until golden and risen. Let cool in the pan for 5 minutes, then transfer to a wire rack to cool completely.

(F) Open freeze on a tray, then place in a plastic bag, label, and return to the freezer.

(D) Place on a wire rack for 4 to 5 hours, then eat as they are or warm in a low oven. Dust with confectioners' sugar to serve.

desserts

nutty honeycomb ice cream

3/4 cup pecans
vegetable oil, for greasing
heaping 1/2 cup superfine sugar
3 tablespoons golden syrup or dark
   corn syrup
1 teaspoon baking soda
2 teaspoons vanilla extract
1 quart heavy cream
1 (14-ounce) can lowfat or regular
   condensed milk

This recipe is an adaptation of a family favorite recipe for honeycomb ice cream, handed down to my sister-in-law Katie from her mom. The addition of nuts makes this my best type of ice cream! Eat it within a couple of weeks, as it tends to lose its texture if you leave it for too long.

Makes about 2 1/2 quarts

Preheat the oven to 375°F. Coarsely break the pecans in your hands, spread them out on a baking sheet, and place in the oven for 5 minutes, or until toasted. Remove from the oven and let cool.

Oil a sheet of wax paper and place on a baking sheet. In a saucepan, place the sugar and syrup and heat gently, swirling the pan until the sugar melts. Turn up the heat and boil until it turns a rich caramel color, watching the mixture all the time to avoid it burning, about 4 minutes. Remove the pan from the heat, then add the nuts and very carefully sprinkle in the baking soda. It will suddenly look frothy and increase in volume. Stir, then pour quickly (before it sets) onto the oiled wax paper. Let cool and set. Transfer to a plastic bag and bash with a rolling pin to break it into smallish chunks.

Using a hand mixer, in a large bowl, whip the cream and vanilla extract until thickened slightly—it should be floppy but should not have reached peaks stage. Then, with the mixer still running, pour in the condensed milk. Continue beating until just stiff. Fold in the pieces of nutty honeycomb plus any crumbs.

(F) Turn into a 3-quart container and freeze for 6 to 8 hours.

(S) Remove from the freezer 20 minutes before you want to eat it and let it start to thaw in a cool place.

Tip: You might need to fill your saucepan with water once you have poured out the honeycomb mixture and bring it to the boil to remove the caramel.

no-churn vanilla ice cream

$2\frac{1}{2}$ cups heavy cream

1 (14-ounce) can lowfat or regular
condensed milk

$1\frac{2}{3}$ cups freshly made Custard Sauce
(see page 30), cooled

$1\frac{1}{2}$ teaspoons vanilla extract

If you are ice-cream lovers like my family and me, then you'll appreciate the simplicity of this recipe—especially the fact that you don't have to churn it! Eat it within a couple of weeks, as it tends to lose its texture if you leave it for too long.

Makes about $1\frac{1}{2}$ quarts

Using a hand mixer, in a large bowl, whip the cream until floppy. With the mixer still running, beat in the condensed milk, custard sauce, and vanilla extract. Continue beating for about a minute.

(F) Pour into a 2-quart freezer container and seal with a lid.

(S) Remove from the freezer 20 minutes before you want to eat it and let it start to thaw in a cool place.

strawberry and meringue ice cream

2³/₄ cups ripe strawberries

3 tablespoons good-quality strawberry jam

1²/₃ cups heavy cream

¹/₂ (14-ounce) can lowfat or regular condensed milk

4 meringue cookies or meringue shells, crushed in your hands

The addition of the jam seems odd, but it really intensifies the strawberry flavor. Eat this within a couple of weeks, as it tends to lose its texture if you leave it for too long.

Makes about 1³/₄ quarts

In a blender, place the strawberries and jam and blend until puréed. Using a hand mixer, whip the cream until floppy. With the beaters still going, beat in the condensed milk and then the strawberry purée. Continue beating until just stiff but still pourable, then fold in the crushed meringues.

(F) Pour into a 2-quart freezer container and seal with a lid.

(S) Remove from the freezer 20 minutes before you want to eat it and let it start to thaw in a cool place.

rhubarb crunch ice cream

18 ounces rhubarb, fresh or frozen, cut into chunks (no need to thaw)
4 tablespoons superfine sugar
2 tablespoons fresh orange juice

For the crunch
$2/3$ cup less 1 tablespoon all-purpose flour
4 tablespoons butter, chilled, diced
3 tablespoons light brown sugar

For the ice cream base
$2^1/2$ cups light cream
1 (14-ounce) can lowfat or regular condensed milk

I couldn't decide whether this was a cheesecake or a crumble, so decided it would be a crunch! Avoid tough, very green rhubarb because it just doesn't have the same flavor. Eat it within a couple of weeks, as it tends to lose its texture if you leave it for too long.

Makes about 2 quarts

Preheat the oven to 350°F. In a baking pan, spread out the rhubarb and sprinkle over the sugar and orange juice. Cover with foil and bake for 25 minutes, or until softened.

Meanwhile, make the crunch. In a bowl, rub the butter into the flour with your fingertips, then stir in the sugar. Spread out onto a $9^1/2$ x 8-inch pan so that it is about $1/2$ inch thick and press down. Bake for about 20 minutes. Remove both fruit and crunch from the oven when cooked and let cool in their pans.

Using a hand mixer, whip the cream in a large bowl until floppy. With the mixer still running, add the condensed milk and any rhubarb cooking juice. Fold in the cooled rhubarb and beat again until thickened but still pourable. Coarsely break up the crumble and fold in, leaving some nice chunky bits.

(F) Turn into a 2-quart freezer container and freeze.

(S) Remove from the freezer 20 minutes before serving.

blue and red ice cream

2^{1}/$_{2}$ cups blueberries

1^{1}/$_{2}$ heaping cups raspberries

4 tablespoons sloe gin or apple juice

1^{1}/$_{2}$ (14-ounce) cans lowfat or regular condensed milk

3 cups plus 2 tablespoons heavy cream

4 meringue cookies or meringue shells, lightly crushed (optional)

I thought it would be nice to make an ice cream with these black and red fruits as together they create the most beautiful colors. You could make this with just blueberries if you like, but a mixture works better. The fruits can be cooked from frozen if you have not bought them fresh. Eat it within a couple of weeks, as it tends to lose its texture if you leave it for too long.

Makes about 2 quarts

In a saucepan, place the blueberries, raspberries, gin, or juice and simmer for 5 to 10 minutes, stirring occasionally. When the fruits look like they have more or less burst, strain through a strainer over a bowl and, using a spatula, push all the purée through. Let the purée cool.

Using a hand mixer, whip the cream until floppy, then beat in the condensed milk and berry purée. Using a spoon, fold in the meringue (if using) and turn into a 2-quart container.

(**F**) Place in the freezer for at least 4 to 5 hours, or until frozen.

(**S**) Remove 20 minutes or so before eating and let stand in a cool place. Turn out onto a plate and cut into slices.

blue and red terrine

$2^{1}/_{2}$ cups blueberries

$1^{1}/_{2}$ heaping cups raspberries

4 tablespoons sloe gin or crème de cassis

$1^{1}/_{2}$ (14-ounce) cans lowfat or regular condensed milk

3 cups plus 2 tablespoons cream

4 meringue cookies or meringue shells, lightly crushed

This is a more glamorous twist on the previous ice cream, and the great news is it doesn't need churning, so you can whip it up in the morning and forget about it until you are ready to serve it. The addition of a shot of booze adds an extra dimension, but you can use just water or apple juice if you prefer. Eat it within a couple of weeks, as it tends to lose its texture if you leave it for too long.

Makes 2 (2-pound) terrines

You will need two (2-pound) loaf pans.

In a saucepan, place the blueberries, raspberries, and sloe gin or crème de cassis with 2 tablespoons water and simmer for 5 to 10 minutes, stirring occasionally. When the berries have all more or less burst, strain them through a strainer over a bowl, using a spatula to push all the purée through.

Using a hand mixer, whip the cream until floppy, then beat in the condensed milk and fruit purée. Using a spoon, fold in the meringue and turn the mixture into 2 nonstick (or plastic wrap-lined) loaf pans.

(**F**) Place in the freezer for at least 4 to 5 hours, or until frozen.

(**S**) Remove 20 minutes or so before eating and let stand in a cool place. Turn out onto a plate, dipping the pans into warm water if sticking, and cut into slices.

mojito sherbet

zest and juice of 8 to 10 limes
(you need $^3/_4$ cup plus 3 tablespoons
lime juice)
$^3/_4$ cup plus 2 tablespoons white
superfine sugar
juice of 1 large lemon
$^1/_3$ cup plus 1 tablespoon white rum
15 large young mint leaves, very
finely chopped

To serve
mint leaves

**What can I say—it's my favorite drink and now I've made it into a dessert!
Don't be tempted to add more alcohol, as it will take forever to freeze
(or, depending on how much you've added, it won't freeze at all!)**

Makes 2$^3/_4$ cups (enough for 4)

In a saucepan, place the lime zest and sugar with $^2/_3$ cup water and heat
gently until dissolved. Let cool for 5 minutes. Meanwhile, juice the limes and
lemon and pour into a pitcher. Add the sugar syrup, rum, and mint and stir.

(F) Pour into a 1-quart container (a tall container is best if you have one;
you can then just insert a hand blender to blend it halfway through) and
freeze for 4 to 5 hours, or until semi-frozen. Beat with a hand blender
or a fork to break up the ice crystals. Return to the freezer. If possible,
beat it again—the more you do, the finer the sherbet will be. Freeze the
sherbet again until frozen.

(S) Remove the sherbet from the freezer just before you want to use it and
serve in little glasses, topped with some extra mint.

pavlova with pomegranates and raspberries

$^3/_4$ cup egg white (about 4 large eggs, but make sure to measure)
$1^3/_4$ cups superfine sugar
2 teaspoons cornstarch
1 teaspoon white wine vinegar

To serve
2 cups pomegranate seeds (about 4 fresh pomegranates)
scant $2^1/_2$ cups raspberries, fresh or frozen
2 tablespoons superfine sugar
$1^1/_4$ cups heavy cream

A billowy pavlova topped with ripe glistening fruits never fails to impress and, what's more, it's a heavenly combination to eat, too! Using frozen raspberries for this is ideal, as they thaw very quickly on the top and they add a burst of summer flavor to a winter menu. You can remove the seeds from fresh pomegranates instead of buying a package of pomegranate seeds if you prefer—cheaper but a little more time consuming.

Serves 6

Preheat the oven to 325°F. Draw a 9-inch circle on a sheet of wax paper, then place the sheet on a large baking sheet.

In a large bowl, using a hand mixer, whip the egg whites on maximum speed until they form shiny stiff peaks. Add 6 teaspoons of the sugar, one straight after the other. Then, with the mixer still beating, add an additional 2 teaspoons every 10 seconds until it is all incorporated. Sprinkle over the cornstarch and vinegar and fold in using a large metal spoon.

Spoon the mixture into the center of the wax paper circle and spread out, leveling the center and building up the side to form peaks or swirls.

As soon as you place the pavlova into the oven, reduce the oven temperature to 300°F and bake for 1 hour. Turn off the oven and let the meringue cool completely while still in the oven, with the door ajar.

(F) Open freeze on the baking sheet, then, if you need to, carefully transfer to a container or bag and cover before refreezing.

(D) Remove from the freezer 2 hours before you want to use it and thaw at room temperature.

(S) While the meringue thaws, in a saucepan, place half the pomegranate seeds and scant $^2/_3$ cup of the raspberries with 2 tablespoons water. Simmer until the raspberries are softened and the mix is a little syrupy. Stir in the sugar, then strain the mixture through a strainer and reserve the sauce. (You can do this ahead and keep in the fridge.) In a bowl, whip the cream and spread over the meringue. Scatter the remaining pomegranate seeds and raspberries over the top. Drizzle over the sauce and serve (or serve the sauce in a pitcher to hand around, if you prefer).

Variations:

Pavlova with strawberries and passion fruit—Make, freeze, and thaw the pavlova following the recipe opposite and fill with $1^1/4$ cups whipped heavy cream. Scatter over $2^3/4$ cups strawberries, halved if large, and the seeds from 2 passion fruit. Decorate with edible flowers, such as rose petals or pansies, if you wish.

Chocolate pavlova—You must use a regular unsweetened cocoa for this rather than an upscale one with a higher fat content, otherwise the mixture collapses. Add $1^1/2$ tablespoons cocoa along with the sugar when making the pavlova.

Individual meringues—To make individual meringues rather than a pavlova, follow the pavlova recipe but reduce the quantity of sugar to $1^1/4$ cups and omit the cornstarch and vinegar. Spoon the mixture in 15 to 20 large, well-spaced mounds onto two baking sheets lined with wax paper. Bake at 225°F for 1 hour 20 minutes, or until the meringue bottoms are crisp and sound hollow when tapped gently. Let cool on the sheets, then transfer to a container and freeze.

fruit puddings

$1^3/_4$ cups red currants
$1^3/_4$ cups blackberries
$2^3/_4$ cups raspberries
heaping $^1/_3$ cup superfine sugar
$1^1/_2$ tablespoons crème de cassis
$1^1/_2$ cups strawberries
8 to 10 medium slices white bread,
    one day old and crusts removed

To serve
whipped cream

My wonderful grandmother Sybil made summer puddings for us when we were children—most, if not all, of the fruit coming from her garden. I've made individual puddings as I think they look so dainty on a plate.

Makes 6

You will need 6 dariole molds.

In a saucepan, place the red currants, blackberries, and half the raspberries with the sugar and crème de cassis and heat gently until the fruit begins to shine and release its juice. Cook until you have a good amount of liquid in the pan but the fruit still retains some texture, about 5 minutes.

Using a rolling pin, roll out the slices of bread to stretch them and make them a bit thinner. Using a cutter the same diameter as the bottom of your molds, cut out 12 circles. Cut the remaining bread slices into strips to fit around the insides of your molds, just reaching the top. Dip one side of each piece of bread into the fruit juices in the pan and fit the circles into the bottom and the strips around the inside of the molds, fruity side outward, leaving six soaked circles on a plate.

Add the remaining raspberries and strawberries to the pan, give them a stir, then divide the fruit and remaining juices among the molds. Top each mold with a circle of soaked bread (fruity side upward) and cover the molds with plastic wrap.

(F) Let stand in the fridge for an hour, then cover each mold with foil and transfer to the freezer.

(D) Let stand at room temperature for about 4 to 6 hours.

(S) Turn the molds out onto plates and serve with whipped cream.

flavored vodkas

I am wondering whether my brother has set up a vodka factory from his home, and whether that's legal! I asked him to kindly investigate some interesting flavors of vodka, as he is a bit of a magician when it comes to experimenting with recipes and cocktails. Anyway, a few weeks later and here they are. All are totally delicious—and all deadly after dinner! They can also all can be stored in the freezer.

pomegranate vodka

Extract the seeds from a pomegranate by cutting in half, holding the cut side in the hollow of your hand, and whacking the back with a rolling pin, then add the seeds to 2 cups vodka and steep for 12 hours. The vodka will go pinkish and take on some of the flavor. Drink as a shot with a few of the frozen seeds in each glass to crunch up as you drink.

strawberry and rose water vodka

Cut $1^{3}/_{4}$ cups ripe strawberries into pieces small enough to fit through the neck of the vodka bottle. Add to 2 cups vodka, then add 2 to 4 teaspoons of rose water and 3 tablespoons simple syrup. Let steep for 24 hours, then strain out the strawberries and place in the freezer. The vodka will be pink.

thai fire vodka

Score 1 lemongrass stalk and 1 green chile with a knife lengthwise (but do not cut in half). Add to an 18-ounce bottle of vodka with a 1-inch piece fresh ginger or galangal, cut into lengths, and 10 fresh or 5 dried kaffir lime leaves, torn. Steep for 12 hours. Store in the freezer. This makes an amazing Bloody Mary and also works well layered with coconut milk in a shot glass.

speedy dishwasher chocolate and mint vodka

Smash up $3^{1}/_{2}$ ounces 70 percent bittersweet chocolate and feed it into a bottle containing $1^{2}/_{3}$ cups vodka. Screw on the cap tightly and place in the dishwasher on a hot cycle. When it's finished, add 2 to 3 teaspoons good-quality mint extract to taste. Shake, cool, and place in the freezer to chill. This recipe also works very well with the zest of 1 orange to replace the mint, or half a seeded scored red chile. And for those with a sweeter chocolate tooth, this method also works brilliantly with chopped up Mars Bars.

dark chocolate mousse

$^2/_3$ cup heavy cream

$^1/_3$ cup plus 1 tablespoon whole milk

2 tablespoons superfine sugar

3 tablespoons Amaretto or brandy

9 ounces good-quality semisweet or
  bittersweet chocolate, broken up

2 large eggs, at room temperature,
  separated

1 teaspoon cornstarch

To serve

8 almond macaroons

unsweetened cocoa, to dust

cream, for pouring

I have been on a mission to discover a foolproof recipe for a freezable chocolate mousse. This one provides endless variations: you could add raspberries to the base and kirsch to the mix, or replace the Amaretto or brandy with a tablespoon of espresso coffee or some orange juice or Cointreau. You could also try using flavored chocolate, such as mint. Keeping the eggs at room temperature helps the chocolate to behave— too cold and the mixture will turn into a thick lump. For even richer mousse, leave out the egg white (makes 6).

Makes 8

In a heavy-bottom pan, place the cream, milk, sugar, and Amaretto or brandy and heat gently until nearly boiling. Remove the pan from the heat, add the chocolate, swirl the pan to coat the chocolate with the cream, and let melt, about 5 minutes.

Meanwhile, in a small bowl, beat the egg yolks and cornstarch together until smooth. Stir the chocolate mixture until smooth, then stir in the egg and cornstarch mixture. Heat gently for 5 minutes, stirring continuously with a wooden spoon. Remove from the heat, pour into a bowl, and let cool for 10 minutes.

In a bowl, whip the egg whites until stiff and fold into the chocolate mixture. Pour the mousse into 8 small pots, cups, or ramekins and chill for 1 hour.

(**F**) When set, cover the pots with plastic wrap and freeze.

(**D**) Remove from the freezer and place in the fridge to thaw gently for 2 hours.

(**S**) Dust the tops of the mousse with unsweetened cocoa and serve with almond macaroons and a pitcher of pouring cream.

ice pops

about $1^2/_3$ cups to $2^1/_2$ cups fruit juice (buy a variety of colors to make stripy ice pops, see opposite)

To serve (optional)

7 ounces semisweet, milk, or white chocolate

colored nonpareils, stars, or chocolate sprinkles

I can never quite work out whether my son is eating something healthy or frightful as he returns from a visit to our local grocery store munching a fruit-flavored ice pop shaped like a cartoon character. I am now trying to make ice pops myself, where possible using some of the fabulous fruit juices and smoothies available. If you have time, make them stripy or decorate them with sprinkles; if not, just keep them simple. Getting the chocolate on can be messy, but it is a fun activity for children.

Makes about 4 (depending on the size of your ice pop molds)

You will need 4 plastic ice pop molds with their plastic lids with sticks attached (or wooden sticks if you prefer the old-fashioned look).

Pour the fruit juice into the ice pop molds until it reaches one third of the way up, then freeze until just set. Once frozen, pour in juice of a contrasting color, then freeze again. When this second layer is semi-frozen, push in the sticks, top up with a third flavor/color, and refreeze until solid. (You can add as many stripes and refreeze as many times as you like, but it's best to push the sticks in when the second layer is still semi-frozen to ensure they are well secured.)

You can either serve the ice pops as they are or decorate them with chocolate and sprinkles. The easiest method I have found is to melt the chocolate in a heatproof bowl over a pan of barely simmering water (or in the microwave), then, using a spoon, drizzle a small amount of chocolate over the end of the unmolded completely frozen ice pop and sprinkle with nonpareils, stars, or chocolate sprinkles. Rest the ice pop in the freezer—on a special ice pop holder if you have one so that the chocolate ends don't get smudged—and refreeze until solid.

syrup, orange, and walnut tart

$1^{1}/_{3}$ cups corn syrup (heat the bottle
in some hot water to loosen the
syrup first)

$3^{1}/_{3}$ cups crustless white Bread
Crumbs (see page 23, direct from
the freezer is fine)

zest and juice of $^{1}/_{2}$ orange

4 tablespoons heavy cream

1 egg, beaten

2 (8-inch) blind-baked sweet pie shells

scant 1 cup walnut pieces or chopped
walnut halves

I make two of these tarts at a time to avoid wastage as one uses only half an egg, half a package of walnuts, and a quarter of an orange. I've made life easy and used ready-made and baked sweet pie shells, but if you like, you can make your own pie dough (see page 28), or buy a fresh block of pie dough, line a couple of flan tins, and blind bake the tart cases yourself (see page 144).

Makes 2 tarts, each serving 6

Preheat the oven to 375°F. Pour the syrup into a smallish saucepan and melt over low heat. Remove the pan from the heat and add the bread crumbs, orange zest and juice, cream, and egg and stir to combine. Pour into the pie shells and scatter with the walnut pieces. Bake for 20 minutes, then cool.

(F) Ideally, leave in the flan pans or foil tart pans to freeze, but if you need to, once cool, you can carefully remove the tarts before covering and freezing them.

(R) To reheat from frozen, place in a preheated oven at 375°F for 15 to 20 minutes until piping hot. If thawed, cook at 300°F for 25 minutes. Cover with foil if the pastry begins to look too dark.

late summer frangipane tart

all-purpose flour, for dusting

12 ounces ($^1/_3$ quantity) Sweet Pie
 Dough (see page 28)

$^3/_4$ cup butter, softened

1$^3/_4$ cups ground almonds

$^3/_4$ cup superfine sugar

3 large eggs

1$^2/_3$ cups raspberries or blackberries
 or blueberries or a mix , frozen
 or fresh

2 tablespoons slivered almonds

This is the perfect prepare-ahead tart: it is stylish, light enough for a dinner party (you can make it in individual cases if you like), and comforting enough to end a Sunday lunch party, too. Using frozen berries means you can enjoy it all year round.

Serves 6 to 8

If using frozen fruits, remove them from the freezer so they can begin to thaw while you prepare the pie dough. Preheat the oven to 375°F.

On a floured counter, roll out the pie dough and use it to line a 9$^1/_2$-inch diameter 1-inch deep loose-bottom tart pan. Scrunch up a piece of wax paper (it makes it easier to fit in the creases) and spread out over the pie dough. Fill with dried beans. Bake for 15 minutes. Remove the paper and beans from the pie shell and return it to the oven for an additional 5 minutes, or until the bottom has dried out. Remove from the oven and let cool.

In a food processor, place the butter, almonds, and sugar and process until combined and creamy, about 20 seconds. Spoon over the pie shell and top with the berries and slivered almonds. Bake for 40 minutes, or until evenly golden. Cool.

(F) Open freeze in its pan, then transfer to a bag and refreeze.

(D) Let stand for about 2 to 4 hours at room temperature.

(R) Place in a preheated oven at 350°F for 10 to 15 minutes.

sticky banana apple puddings with toffee sauce

$^1/_2$ cup pecans

2 very ripe bananas (blackened is best)

2 large eggs

$1^1/_2$ tablespoons whole plain yogurt

1 small (5$^1/_2$-ounce) apple, peeled, cored, and shredded

$^1/_3$ cup golden raisins

6 tablespoons butter, melted

heaping $^1/_2$ cup light brown sugar

$^1/_2$ teaspoon ground cinnamon

$1^1/_2$ cups self-rising flour

$1^1/_2$ level teaspoons baking powder

$^3/_4$ teaspoon baking soda

For the toffee sauce

$^3/_4$ cup plus 2 tablespoons light brown sugar

4 tablespoons butter

$1^1/_4$ cups heavy cream

An alternative version of the sticky toffee pudding we all know and love, this has a hint of healthiness about it until you drown it in the toffee sauce!

You will need 8 dariole molds or mini bowls.

Preheat the oven to 350°F. Grease the dariole molds or mini bowls.

Scatter the pecans on a baking sheet and toast for about 5 minutes in the oven. Remove to a board and, when cool, coarsely chop.

In a large bowl, mash the bananas with a fork. Add the eggs, yogurt, shredded apple, chopped nuts, golden raisins, melted butter, sugar, and cinnamon and mix together using the fork until thoroughly combined. Sift over the flour, baking powder, and baking soda. Using a large metal spoon, fold in gently until only just combined. Divide among the molds and bake for 20 to 30 minutes, or until brown and cooked through. (Insert a skewer into the center of one of the cakes to see if it comes out clean. If there is cake stuck to it, bake for a few minutes more.) Let cool slightly while you make the sauce.

In a saucepan, place the sugar and butter and stir over low heat until dissolved. Add the cream and simmer for 2 to 3 minutes until richly colored. Remove from the heat and pour into a container. When the cakes are done, let them cool in their molds slightly, then remove them by sliding a knife around the edges and transfer them to a wire rack to cool completely.

(F) Open freeze the cakes, then put them in bags, label, and refreeze. Freeze the sauce in the container, covered.

(D) Leave for about 4 to 5 hours at room temperature.

(R) Warm the sauce slightly in a saucepan or the microwave, then pour half into the bottom of a baking dish. Sit the puddings on top and spoon over the remaining sauce. Cover with foil and bake in a preheated oven at 350°F for 15 minutes, or until piping hot and bubbling.

christmas turnovers

about 1 tablespoon butter

1 large (7-ounce) baking apple, peeled, cored, and chopped

1 large (6-ounce) pear, peeled, cored, and chopped

$1^1/_2$ tablespoons raw brown sugar

2 heaping tablespoons golden raisins

$^1/_4$ teaspoon ground cinnamon

splash of brandy (optional)

1 (14-ounce) box refrigerated ready-rolled puff pastry

all-purpose flour, for dusting

1 egg, beaten

superfine sugar, for sprinkling

Whether made with rhubarb, blackberry and apple, or a mix of whatever I've got in the fruit bowl, I love a turnover, especially served straight from the oven with a large spoonful of cream! They look just as at home on the children's dessert table with ice cream as they do at a dinner party dusted with confectioners' sugar and served with thick cream.

Makes 6

In a saucepan, place the butter, apple, pear, sugar, golden raisins, cinnamon, and brandy (if using) and simmer, stirring occasionally, until the apples and pears are soft and mushy, about 15 minutes. Remove the pan from the heat and let cool.

Unroll the sheet of pastry and place on a floured counter. Roll the pastry out so you can cut out six $4^1/_4$-inch circles. Brush around the rim of the dough circles with the beaten egg. Spoon about a tablespoon of the filling onto one half of each circle, avoiding the egg-brushed rim, then fold over the pastry and press to seal. Use the end of a spoon to press down around the edges to ensure a good seal and avoid leakages. Brush the turnovers all over with beaten egg, sprinkle with sugar, and place on a plate covered with wax paper.

(F) Open freeze the turnovers, then transfer to a bag, label, and refreeze.

(C) Cook from frozen in a preheated oven at 400°F for 25 to 30 minutes, or until golden.

oat crumble

3²/₃ cups all-purpose flour
1²/₃ cups butter, chilled, diced
1 cup plus 2 tablespoons raw brown sugar
1¹/₂ cups superfine sugar
2 heaping cups rolled oats

The best machine for a quick crumble mix is in fact a stand mixer. It's a hassle to get out of the cabinet, but it means you can put everything in together and make a big batch in one go—plus it produces a really good "handmade" texture rather than the powder that can result from using a food processor. If you prefer, of course, you can make it the good old-fashioned way and rub the butter into the flour with your fingertips before adding the rest of the ingredients.

For approximately 12 to 14 portions

In a stand mixer fitted with the paddle attachment, place all the ingredients, distributing the pieces of butter throughout. Mix at a medium speed until the mixture looks crumbly (biggish bread crumbs is the simplest description). Pour into a bag or container.

F Seal the bag or the container, label, and freeze.

C Sprinkle on top of the fruits of your choice (I like to soften them a little first over gentle heat, with a little butter, sweetening if required) and press down lightly. Cook in a preheated oven at 350°F for 30 to 40 minutes, or until golden and bubbling.

raspberry and apple crumble

2 tablespoons butter

18 ounces frozen baking apple slices (or 3 medium baking apples, cored, peeled, and sliced)

3 tablespoons raw brown sugar

1$^2/_3$ cups raspberries, fresh or frozen

4 to 6 handfuls Oat Crumble (see page 147) or enough to completely cover the fruit

To serve

ice cream

Just double the quantities and use a bigger dish for larger numbers, cooking for a little longer. If using your own frozen apple slices, you will probably need to thaw them slightly first as they can form a clump!

Serves 4

Preheat the oven to 350°F.

In a saucepan, melt the butter and add the apples. Toss together for 2 to 3 minutes over the heat, then sprinkle in the sugar and add the frozen berries (if using fresh berries, add them right at the end of cooking). Stir over the heat until the raspberries are just beginning to turn the apples pinkish, then pour into a baking dish, patting down to fill in any gaps. Scatter over the crumble mix and bake for 30 to 40 minutes, or until golden and bubbling. Serve with ice cream.

Variations:

Summer berry—Use a mixture of different summer berries, frozen or fresh, in place of the raspberries. Or use 1$^3/_4$ pounds mixed berries on their own, and reduce the sugar to 1$^1/_2$ tablespoons. Soften the berries in a pan until they start to release their juice.

Rhubarb—Substitute the apple and raspberries with 21 ounces frozen or fresh rhubarb chunks.

Apricot and apple—Use a can of apricots in juice in place of the raspberries. Add the apricots, along with about half their juice, to the apples after you have softened and sweetened them.

babies and children

feeding babies and toddlers

This will, I hope, make weaning and feeding babies and toddlers easier for busy parents. Weaning should be an exciting time, but as you may never have made purées before and you will want to make sure you are doing it right, it can feel like the pressure is on. The best advice is to keep it simple. And remember a baby has never tasted apple or carrot before, so although it seems rather basic to us, it's a whole new world of taste for them and it may take a few attempts before your baby enjoys it.

This is where a freezer is a lifesaver if you are a new parent: it enables you to make batches of different purées and freeze them in ice cube trays, then introduce them slowly, rather than spending hours in the kitchen lovingly preparing something, only to have to throw it away when your child rejects it! A microwave is also a great help, if you use one, as is a hand blender.

You will want to wean your baby your own way, and every child is different, so I'm not going to attempt to give serving amounts or a routine for when to introduce new flavors. I haven't included everything, as there's not enough space, and in any case, I am sure you can work out how to boil a carrot or mash a banana! However, the first-stage combinations that follow have all been favorites with my children and hopefully will provide some inspiration for you, too.

I have also included some easy-to-freeze dishes, such as Cauliflower Cheese and Pizza, that are suitable for toddlers but that I hope will be loved by all the family. Conversely, many of the recipes throughout the rest of book are also very baby and toddler friendly. You may just want to adjust the quantities of salt and sugar in the recipes if you are feeding young children.

first stages purées

apple and pear purée

2 apples, such as Braeburn
2 ripe pears (3 if small)

This was the first thing I introduced with both my children. You can mix it with a little infant rice to mellow the flavor a little.

Makes about 20 cubes

Peel and core the fruits, then slice into a pan or microwave-safe bowl. Add a tiny dash of water, then simmer gently for 5 to 8 minutes, or steam, until the fruits are soft. Alternatively, cover the bowl with plastic wrap, pierce a few times, and microwave until soft and mushy, 4 to 8 minutes. Purée.

(F) Spoon the purée into ice cube trays and let cool, then freeze. Once frozen, transfer the cubes into a labeled freezer bag.

(S) Thaw, or warm through from frozen if you like.

pear and mango purée

2 ripe pears (3 if small)
2 ripe mangoes

This purée is uncooked, so ideal for a last-minute quick dessert.

Makes about 20 cubes

Peel the fruits and slice into a bowl. Purée until smooth.

(F) Spoon the purée into ice cube trays and let cool, then freeze. Once frozen, transfer the cubes into a labeled freezer bag.

(S) Thaw, or warm through from frozen if you like.

apple and blackberry purée

2 apples, such as Braeburn
1 heaping cup blackberries

This one goes well with some infant rice or, when your baby is a little older, with some creamy rice pudding or custard sauce mixed in. Soft rice is an ideal first texture.

Makes about 20 cubes

Peel the apples, quarter and core, then slice into a pan or bowl. Add the blackberries and a dash of water, then simmer gently for 5 to 8 minutes until soft. Alternatively, cover the (microwave-safe) bowl with plastic wrap, pierce a few times, and microwave until soft (watch it though as it does have a tendency to boil over), 4 to 6 minutes. Purée.

(F) Spoon the purée into ice cube trays and let cool, then freeze. Once frozen, transfer the cubes into a labeled freezer bag.

(S) Thaw, or warm through from frozen if you like.

bell pepper and sweet potato purée

12 ounces sweet potato, peeled and cut into chunks
$3^{1}/_{2}$ ounces fresh or frozen sliced mixed bell peppers or $3^{1}/_{2}$ ounces red bell pepper, seeded and chopped
splash of cooking water, or some milk and about 1 tablespoon butter if your baby is at this stage

Using frozen bell pepper slices is just as nutritious and a quick way to rustle up a batch of purée.

Makes about 12 cubes

Boil the sweet potato for 15 minutes, then add the frozen bell pepper, bring back to a boil, and continue to cook for 5 minutes. (If you are using fresh bell pepper, add it 5 minutes earlier and make sure it is soft before draining.) Drain, reserving a little of the cooking water if needed, and blend until completely puréed (make sure there are no stray bits of pepper skin as babies don't really like this!). Stir in milk and butter or a splash of the cooking water to loosen if necessary.

(F) Spoon into ice cube trays, cool, and freeze, then transfer to a freezer bag, label, and refreeze.

(S) Reheat. You can cook from frozen if you like.

beet and carrot puree

7 ounces carrots, peeled and cut
  into chunks
3 peeled, cooked beets, cut into chunks
4 tablespoons milk or cooking water

My daughter Jemima loves this as it's so sweet. The beets also turn the puree the most stunning vivid pink! I often combine it with mashed potatoes. If your baby is at the right stage, you can also cook the vegetables in chicken stock for more flavor. Use fresh cooked beets if you have some on hand (boil the unpeeled beets for about 25 minutes, or until soft, then peel), or precooked beets in natural juice.

Makes about 14 cubes

Boil the carrots in water for about 15 minutes, or until tender. Strain, reserving some of the cooking water, then add the beets and puree. Add the milk or cooking water to loosen.

(**F**) Spoon the puree into ice cube trays and let cool, then freeze. Once frozen, transfer the cubes into a labeled freezer bag.

(**S**) Reheat. You can cook from frozen if you like.

first chicken four ways

4 chicken legs, skin removed from all but 1

1 large leek, trimmed and thickly sliced

2 medium potatoes, peeled and cut into large chunks

1 large carrot, peeled and cut into large chunks

8 ounces butternut squash, peeled, seeded, and cut into large chunks

$1/2$ cup dry pasta stars or other small pasta shapes

$1/2$ (7-ounce) can corn kernels with no added salt or sugar, or 1 corn on the cob, cooked and kernels removed

heaping $1/2$ cup frozen peas, thawed

2 to 3 tablespoons milk, if needed

I developed this recipe when weaning my second child, Jemima. No longer was there time for individual this and that! Adapt the recipe to suit you, your child's likes and dislikes, and the vegetables you have in your pantry or fridge. If your baby doesn't like lumps, then purée everything, otherwise add the pasta to the chicken and vegetables once puréed to add some texture. You can also make a small quantity of white sauce or add shredded cheese if you want to vary things a little more.

Makes about 4 large ice cube trays, 1 each of the following:

chicken with carrot, potato, and corn
chicken with potatoes, peas, and butternut squash
chicken pasta with butternut squash and corn
chicken pasta with peas and carrots

In a pot, place the chicken legs and leek with 1 quart cold water and slowly bring to a boil. Reduce to a simmer and cook for 30 minutes, then, using a slotted spoon, remove the chicken and leeks to a board to cool. Add the potato, carrot, and butternut squash to the boiling stock. Cook until all the vegetables are tender, about 20 minutes, then strain and set aside. Meanwhile, cook the pasta in a separate pan, strain, and rinse.

Divide the leek among 4 bowls. Remove the meat from the chicken legs, discarding any remaining skin and fat, and divide among the bowls. Then divide the remaining ingredients among the 4 bowls as follows:

Bowl a: half the potato, half the carrot, half the corn kernels
Bowl b: half the potato, half the thawed peas, half the butternut squash
Bowl c: half the corn kernels, half the butternut squash
Bowl d: half the carrots, half the thawed peas

Add a little of the stock, or a mix of stock and milk, to each bowl. Blend the contents of each bowl separately, then add extra stock as needed (the ones containing potato will probably need more). Divide the pasta among bowls c and d (i.e. the ones not containing potato) and purée or leave as is.

(F) Spoon the four purées into separate ice cube trays and freeze, then transfer to freezer bags and label.

(S) Thaw, then warm through until piping hot, adding a little milk or water to loosen if necessary.

first fish four ways

1 pound haddock or cod fillet, skin on

2 cups milk

1 medium leek, trimmed and thickly sliced

2 smallish potatoes, peeled and cut into chunks

3¹/₂ ounces frozen leaf spinach (do not used chopped)

1¹/₂ cups broccoli florets

1 small carrot, scrubbed and sliced

1 medium zucchini, trimmed and cut into chunks

1 cup dry pasta stars or other small pasta shapes

1 (7-ounce) can corn kernels, drained, or 1 large corn on the cob, cooked and kernels removed

2 tablespoons butter

1¹/₂ tablespoons all-purpose flour

2 tablespoons shredded cheddar cheese (optional)

The same concept as the chicken recipe on page 156. Although the recipe seems quite a lot of work, in the long run it will save you lots of time and give you a freezer full of varied meals for your baby.

Makes about 4 large ice cube trays, 1 each of the following:

fish, corn, spinach, and potato
fish, zucchini, spinach, and potato
fish, zucchini, corn, cheese, and pasta
fish, broccoli, leek, pasta, and cheese

In a deep skillet or sauté pan, place the milk and leeks and bring to a simmer. Simmer for 7 minutes, then add the fish, skin-side down, and poach for 4 minutes. Turn the fish over and poach for an additional 3 minutes, then turn off the heat and transfer the fish and leeks to a plate using a spatula or slotted spoon. Pour the poaching milk into a pitcher.

While the fish cooks, steam the potato chunks for 5 minutes, then add the spinach to the water underneath and the broccoli, carrot, and zucchini to the steamer (try to keep them separate as it will be easier for later). Steam for an additional 5 to 7 minutes. In a separate small pan, cook the pasta until soft, strain, and rinse.

Now make the white sauce. Melt the butter over low heat (you can use the pasta pan), then add the flour and stir with a wooden spoon. Gradually stir in the poaching milk and simmer for 2 minutes. Season with black pepper and pour into a pitcher.

Remove the skin from the fish and discard, then check for stray bones and divide the cooked fish and white sauce evenly among 4 bowls. Add the vegetables to the bowls as follows:

Bowl a: half the leeks, all the broccoli, 1 tablespoon cheese (if using)
Bowl b: half the leeks, all the zucchini, half the corn kernels
Bowl c: half the potato, all the spinach, 1 tablespoon cheese (if using)
Bowl d: half the potato, all the carrot, half the corn kernels

Blend the contents of each bowl separately. Divide the pasta among bowls a and b (i.e. the ones not containing potato) after blending (or before if your child prefers a smooth purée).

(F) Spoon the four purées into separate ice cube trays and freeze, then transfer to freezer bags and label.

(S) Thaw, then warm through until piping hot, adding a little milk or water to loosen if necessary. Cool until it is the correct temperature.

two potato mash

2 medium sweet potatoes, peeled and cut into 2-inch chunks
1 medium white potato, peeled and cut into 2-inch chunks
milk and about 1 tablespoon butter (optional)

Children love the flavor of sweet potato and this mash is a great thing to have in the freezer to combine with other food, such as some flaked fish or puréed carrot or broccoli.

Makes about 18 to 20 ice cubes

Bring a pan of water to a boil and add the sweet and white potato chunks. Boil for 15 to 25 minutes until softened, then drain, reserving a little water.

Mash the potato (or put through a ricer or purée it if your baby objects to any texture), adding a little of the reserved cooking water or, if your baby is at a slightly later stage of weaning, some milk and butter.

(F) Spoon the mash into ice cube trays or small jars (for toddlers), cool, and then freeze. Once frozen, transfer to freezer bags and label.

(S) Warm through from frozen, adding a little milk, formula, or water to loosen if needed.

pizza

1 (18-ounce) package ciabatta bread mix
1 tablespoon olive oil (or quantity specified in bread mix), plus 2 tablespoons for the top
white bread flour, for dusting
4 to 5 heaping tablespoons All-Purpose Tomato Sauce (see page 33), or a good-quality store-bought tomato sauce
1 teaspoon dried oregano
2 (4$^{1}/_{2}$-ounce) packages fresh mozzarella cheese, drained

Topping suggestions:
My children's favorite—ham, corn, chopped bell pepper, olives, and zucchini
Quattro Stagioni—artichokes, black olives, sliced mushrooms, and strips of fully cooked ham
Fiery—dried red pepper flakes, pepperoni slices, and bell pepper strips
Veggie—roasted bell pepper strips, blanched asparagus spears, and finely sliced zucchini

I have to thank my great friend Kate Titford for opening my eyes to pizza making—using an Italian bread mix as a base suddenly transformed what I used to think was always a rather spongy end result into seriously good crispy pizza. My children adore sprinkling on their own toppings, and these are perfect for that—especially to make ahead for a children's party. Make smaller circles if you'd like them to have one each. However, they are also a huge temptation on a Sunday evening when you get the munchies!

Makes 2 large pizzas, each big enough to serve 2 to 3 adults or 4 children

In a bowl, mix the bread mix according to the package directions. (The one I use says to mix in about 1$^{1}/_{2}$ cups lukewarm water and knead for 5 minutes, then add a tablespoon olive oil and knead for an additional minute, but yours may vary slightly.) Once you have a mixed and kneaded ball of dough, and it no longer feels sticky, cut it into 2 equal pieces, place in a large baking dish, and cover with plastic wrap. Let stand in a warm place (for instance, an oven that has been turned off but is still warm) until it has doubled in size, about 30 minutes.

Remove one of the balls of dough from the dish and place it on a floured counter. Using your hands, covered in a little flour, knead the dough on the counter to remove the air, reshape to a circle, and roll out thinly to a larger circle about 12 to 14 inches in diameter. Place on a nonstick baking sheet. Repeat with the other dough ball and lay out on another sheet.

Spoon 2 to 3 tablespoons tomato sauce into the center of each of the pizzas and spread nearly to the edges. Sprinkle each pizza with $^{1}/_{2}$ teaspoon oregano and a good grinding of pepper. Then tear each mozzarella ball into pieces, dry off with paper towels, and scatter over each pizza.

(F) Open freeze on the baking sheets, then remove to a bag or stack between layers of wax paper and cover tightly with plastic wrap.

(D) For best results, thaw for 3 to 4 hours at room temperature, but you can cook from frozen if you don't have time—just don't overload with toppings or the center will be a bit soggy.

(C) Preheat the oven to 425°F and place 2 baking sheets in the oven at the same time. Top the pizzas with the toppings of your choice, then drizzle with a tablespoon or so of extra virgin olive oil. Transfer to the preheated baking sheets and bake for 10 to 15 minutes if thawed or 15 to 20 minutes from frozen.

cheesy spinach and pea pasta

1 cup dry pasta stars or other small
   pasta shapes
$1^2/_3$ cups whole milk, plus extra to
   loosen if needed
$^1/_3$ cup plus 1 tablespoon all-purpose
   flour
4 tablespoons butter
$3^1/_2$ ounces frozen leaf spinach or fresh
   cooked spinach, drained
$^3/_4$ cup frozen peas
$^1/_2$ cup shredded sharp cheddar cheese

A great suppertime recipe. You can purée the pasta if your baby is not quite at the lumps stage, or cook larger pasta for toddlers and use the same sauce. We also use this sauce as a topping for pasta bakes and lasagna, as it's a great way of disguising vegetables for fussy eaters!

Makes about 20 to 24 ice cubes

In a pot, cook the pasta in plenty of boiling water (give it a stir at intervals to prevent it from sticking), following the package directions for timing, then strain and rinse in cold water.

Meanwhile, in a saucepan, place the milk, flour, and butter and beat over low heat until the butter has melted and the sauce begins to thicken. Add the spinach and peas and, using a wooden spoon, stir over medium heat until both have thawed. Simmer for 5 minutes, then lightly season with pepper and add the cheese (don't worry if it looks a bit thick, as it loosens when you blend it). Purée in a blender, then stir in the pasta, adding a little extra milk to loosen if needed.

(F) Spoon into ice cube trays and freeze, then transfer to a bag and label.

(S) Thaw and reheat, or warm from frozen if you like, adding a little milk
   to loosen if needed.

pasta under the sea

12 ounces dry pasta shapes

1 leek, trimmed and chopped

2 (6-ounce) cans tuna or red (sockeye) salmon, drained

2 (7-ounce) cans corn kernels, drained

For the cheese sauce

2 tablespoons butter

3 tablespoons all-purpose flour

$1^{1}/_{2}$ cups whole milk

$^{1}/_{2}$ cup shredded cheddar cheese

For the top

$^{1}/_{2}$ cup shredded cheddar cheese

handful of cherry tomatoes, halved, or 2 tomatoes, sliced

It's one we've probably all made in our youth, but I had rather forgotten how delicious it was until digging in at a friend's house recently. The children loved it, too! Variations are obviously endless—try adding cooked bacon, chicken, ham, sausage, or spinach to the sauce in place of the canned fish and corn.

Serves 4 adults or 8 children

Cook the pasta according to the package directions, adding the leeks for the final 3 to 4 minutes, then drain, reserving some of the cooking water.

Meanwhile, make the cheese sauce. In a saucepan, place the butter, flour, and milk over gentle heat and beat together with some seasoning until the butter has melted and the sauce thickened. (Make sure to scrape around the edge of the pan with a wooden spoon to prevent the sauce from thickening unevenly.) Bring the sauce to a boil, then add the shredded cheese and simmer for 2 minutes.

Mix with the pasta, leeks, and corn and add enough pasta water to loosen it (it is better to err on the side of runny rather than thick as the pasta will absorb quite a bit of the sauce on cooling). Let cool, then stir in the drained tuna or salmon.

Pour into whichever size dishes you find practical, then top with the remaining cheese and the halved cherry tomatoes or tomato slices.

(**F**) Cover the dishes, label, and freeze.

(**D**) Let stand overnight in the fridge.

(**R**) Preheat the oven to 350°F. Cover the dish with foil, then bake for about 20 to 30 minutes (depending on size) until piping hot. Place under a hot broiler for 5 minutes to brown the top.

mini hamburgers with honey glaze

2 teaspoons vegetable oil
$^1/_2$ red onion, very finely chopped
14 ounces fresh ground beef
pinch of dried oregano
$^1/_2$ teaspoon English mustard powder
$1^1/_2$ teaspoons ketchup
1 teaspoon Worcestershire sauce

To serve
4 teaspoons honey
small hamburger buns, corn on the
   cob, baked beans, french fries

Great for adults and children—the mixture can be made into big or mini hamburgers. If cooking on the barbecue, adjust the cooking time accordingly. For the best results, use fresh ground beef that has not been previously frozen, as you will be freezing the raw hamburgers.

Makes 8 mini hamburgers

In a small skillet, heat the oil, then add the onion and stir over medium heat until softened. Let cool completely.

In a bowl, place the ground beef, oregano, mustard powder, ketchup, and Worcestershire sauce and season with salt and pepper (don't skip the salt completely or the hamburgers will be tasteless). Mix it all together, then, using your hands, shape into 8 mini hamburgers.

(**F**) Place on a sheet of wax paper on a tray or chopping board, then open freeze. Once frozen, transfer to a freezer bag, label, and freeze.

(**R**) Place the frozen hamburgers under a preheated broiler for about 5 minutes, then turn them over and cook for an additional 5 minutes, or until cooked through. Warm the honey to loosen slightly. Brush the hamburgers with the honey, then return them to the broiler for 1 to 2 minutes more to glaze. Serve in hamburger buns or with corn on the cob, baked beans, or french fries.

cauliflower and broccoli cheese with ham and tomatoes

14 ounces broccoli florets (about
  1 large head)
14 ounces cauliflower florets (about
  1 smallish head)
2 cups plus 1 tablespoon whole milk
$^1/_3$ cup butter
scant $^2/_3$ cup all-purpose flour
heaping 1 cup shredded cheddar
  cheese
3 to 4 tablespoons grated Parmesan
  cheese
4 thick slices fully cooked ham, cut
  into strips
15 cherry tomatoes, halved,
  or 4 tomatoes, sliced

An old one but a good one—and the perfect comforting Saturday lunch for the whole family when you don't fancy soup again! It's also heaven with roast chicken (just omit the ham). I tend to freeze it in a mix of little pots for my children, and a bigger dish for a shared lunch.

Serves 4 adults or 8 children

Steam the cauliflower in a large steamer until tender but still with a bite (you will be reheating it, so the vegetables need to still be a bit crunchy at this stage), 8 to 10 minutes. Add the broccoli for the final 5 minutes of cooking time (or, if your steamer is small, steam it separately).

Meanwhile, in a saucepan, place the milk, butter, flour, and some salt and pepper and beat over medium heat until thickened. Simmer for 2 to 3 minutes, then stir in half the cheddar and Parmesan.

Divide the cooked vegetables among whichever size dishes you find practical and scatter over the ham. Pour over the sauce, coating all the vegetables, then scatter with the tomatoes. Let cool for 5 minutes or so, then sprinkle over the remaining cheese.

(**F**) Cool completely, then cover, label, and freeze.

(**D**) Let stand overnight in the fridge. (If using little pots, I tend to just reheat from frozen in the microwave, then finish under the broiler.)

(**R**) Bake, covered in a foil, in a preheated oven at 350°F for about 25 minutes (depending on size), then remove the foil and cook for an additional 10 to 15 minutes until golden brown and bubbling.

sticky chicken

10 chicken drumsticks, skin on,
  slashed 2 or 3 times
4 tablespoons orange juice
  (about 1 orange, juiced)
2 teaspoons grainy mustard
2 teaspoons chopped fresh rosemary
2 teaspoons soy sauce
1½ tablespoons runny honey

Children seem to love getting their teeth into things from a very early age—especially foods like corn on the cob, small sausages, and chicken drumsticks. This is a great recipe, as you can make a large amount, freeze in smaller bags, and then take them out as and when you need them.

Makes 10 drumsticks

Place the chicken drumsticks in a bag (or 2 or 3 bags if you want to freeze it in smaller quantities). In a bowl, mix all the other ingredients together with some ground pepper. Pour into the bag or bags, then knot and shake the chicken around to coat thoroughly in the marinade.

(F) Label the bags and place in the freezer.

(D) Let stand for about 6 to 8 hours in the fridge.

(C) Preheat the oven to 375°F. Place the chicken and marinade in an oiled baking dish, just big enough to fit the drumsticks side by side. Cook for 15 minutes, then turn the drumsticks over and return to the oven for an additional 15 minutes, or until browned and cooked through.

fish pie with hidden vegetables

10 1/2 ounces skinless salmon fillet

10 1/2 ounces skinless cod fillet

1 2/3 cups whole milk

2 heaping cups small broccoli florets

1/2 cup shredded cheddar cheese (optional)

For the vegetable mash

14 ounces potatoes, peeled and cut into chunks

1 large carrot, peeled and cut into chunks

1 medium parsnip, peeled and cut into chunks

2 tablespoons butter

2/3 cup whole milk

For the sauce

4 tablespoons butter

1/2 onion, very finely chopped

2 heaping tablespoons all-purpose flour

This is a great freezable dish for babies and toddlers, as the fish and mash are very mushable for smaller ones or can be kept chunky for bigger children and adults. It has as many vegetables crammed in as possible!

Makes 8 to 10 toddler or 4 adult portions

In a deep skillet or sauté pan, place the fish and milk and bring to a simmer, then reduce the heat slightly and poach with the lid until the fish is just cooked through, 6 to 8 minutes. Pour the milk into a pitcher and flake the fish into your chosen dishes, or 1 large dish, checking for stray bones.

Meanwhile, boil the potatoes, carrots, and parsnips until soft, 15 to 20 minutes. Steam the broccoli on top for the final 5 minutes (or you can boil it if you prefer). Drain the potatoes, carrots, and parsnips and mash with the 2 tablespoons butter and milk. Season with salt and pepper if you like. Scatter the broccoli on top of the flaked fish in the dishes, as small as you like.

To make the sauce, in a saucepan, heat the butter and sauté the onion over gentle heat until softened. Add the flour, stir in, then gradually incorporate the reserved poaching milk. Season, if you like, then simmer until thickened, 2 to 3 minutes. Pour over the fish and broccoli and top with the mash. Scatter with the shredded cheese, if using.

(**F**) Cool, then cover, label, and freeze.

(**D**) Let stand in the fridge overnight (if large), or for 2 to 3 hours (if in small pots).

(**C**) Preheat the oven to 375°F. Uncover the pie and bake for 20 to 35 minutes, depending on the size of the dish, until golden and bubbling.

conversion chart

Weight (solids)

7g = $^1/_4$ oz
10g = $^1/_2$ oz
20g = $^3/_4$ oz
25g = 1 oz
40g = $1^1/_2$ oz
50g = 2 oz
60g = $2^1/_2$ oz
75g = 3oz
100g = $3^1/_2$ oz
110g = 4oz ($^1/_4$ lb)
125g = $4^1/_2$ oz
150g = $5^1/_2$ oz
175g = 6oz
200g = 7oz
225g = 8oz ($^1/_2$ lb)
250g = 9oz
275g = 10oz
300g = $10^1/_2$ oz
310g = 11oz
325g = $11^1/_2$ oz
350g = 12oz ($^3/_4$ lb)
375g = 13oz
400g = 14oz

425g = 15oz
450g = 1lb
500g ($^1/_2$ kg) = 18oz
600g = $1^1/_4$ lb
700g = $1^1/_2$ lb
750g = 1lb 10oz
900g = 2lb
1kg = $2^1/_4$ lb
1.1kg = $2^1/_2$ lb
1.2kg = 2lb 12oz
1.3kg = 3lb
1.5kg = 3lb 5oz
1.6kg = $3^1/_2$ lb
1.8kg = 4lb
2kg = 4lb 8oz
2.25kg = 5lb
2.5kg = 5lb 8oz
3kg = 6lb 8oz

Volume (liquids)

5ml = 1 teaspoon
10ml = 2 teaspoons
15ml = 1 tablespoon
  or $^1/_2$ fl oz

30ml = 1fl oz
40ml = $1^1/_2$ fl oz
50ml = 2fl oz
60ml = $2^1/_2$ fl oz
75ml = 3fl oz
100ml = $3^1/_2$ fl oz
125ml = 4fl oz
150ml = 5fl oz ($^1/_4$ pint)
160ml = $5^1/_2$ fl oz
175ml = 6fl oz
200ml = 7fl oz
225ml = 8fl oz
250ml (0.25 liter) = 9fl oz
300ml = 10fl oz ($^1/_2$ pint)
325ml = 11fl oz
350ml = 12fl oz
370ml = 13fl oz
400ml = 14fl oz
425ml = 15fl oz ($^3/_4$ pint)
450ml = 16fl oz
500ml (0.5 liter) = 18fl oz
550ml = 19fl oz
600ml = 20fl oz (1 pint)
700ml = $1^1/_4$ pints

850ml = $1^1/_2$ pints
1 liter = $1^3/_4$ pints
1.2 liters = 2 pints
1.5 liters = $2^1/_2$ pints
1.8 liters = 3 pints
2 liters = $3^1/_2$ pints

Length

5mm = $^1/_4$ inch
1cm = $^1/_2$ inch
2cm = $^3/_4$ inch
2.5cm = 1 inch
3cm = $1^1/_4$ inches
4cm = $1^1/_2$ inches
5cm = 2 inches
7.5 cm = 3 inches
10cm = 4 inches
15cm = 6 inches
18cm = 7 inches
20cm = 8 inches
24cm = 10 inches
28cm = 11 inches
30 cm = 12 inches

oven temperatures

Celsius*	Farenheit	Gas	Description
110°C	225°F	Gas Mark $^1/_4$	cool
120°C	250°F	Gas Mark $^1/_2$	cool
130°C	275°F	Gas Mark 1	very low
150°C	300°F	Gas Mark 2	very low
160°C	325°F	Gas Mark 3	low
180°C	350°F	Gas Mark 4	moderate
190°C	375°F	Gas Mark 5	moderately hot
200°C	400°F	Gas Mark 6	hot
220°C	425°F	Gas Mark 7	hot
230°C	450°F	Gas Mark 8	very hot
240°C	475°F	Gas Mark 9	very hot

* For fan-assisted ovens, reduce temperatures by 20°C

index

all-in-one white sauce 22

all-purpose tomato sauce 33

apples 12, 14

  apple and blackberry purée 154

  apple and pear purée 153

  applesauce 18

  blackberry and apple crumble 148

  Christmas turnovers 146

  healthier granola bars 106

  pork chops with mustard, apples,
    and cider 72

  sticky banana apple puddings with
    toffee sauce 145

aromatic lamb curry 97

Asian beef skewers 62

asparagus 12

  asparagus and pea risotto 74

avocado

  crab cakes with citrus and avocado
    salad 88

baby food 7, 8, 12, 152

bacon 12

  bacon, cheddar, and sunflower
    squares 113

  finnan haddie chowder 51

  game terrine with pink peppercorns
    55

bananas

  sticky banana apple puddings with
    toffee sauce 145

beef 12

  Asian beef skewers 62

  beef and spinach lasagna 98

  beef wellington 80

  mini hamburgers with honey glaze
    164

  ox cheeks with red wine and
    mushrooms 99

beet and carrot purée 155

berries 12

  frosting 105

  healthier granola bars 106

  summer berry crumble 148

blackberries 14

  apple and blackberry purée 154

  blackberry and apple crumble 148

  late summer frangipane tart 144

black currants

  black and red ice cream 128

  black and red terrine 130

  fruit cage puddings 136

blueberry, almond, and orange
  cupcakes 111

bread 12, 13

  bread sauce 23

  bread crumbs 23

  garlic bread 38

  gazpacho 47

broccoli 14

  cauliflower and broccoli cheese
    with ham and tomatoes 166

buttercream sponge 107

butternut squash 12, 14

  coconut, chicken, and butternut
    squash curry 66

  velvety butternut squash soup 48

cakes 12

  blueberry, almond, and orange
    cupcakes 111

  buttercream sponge 107

  choca-mocha loaf with mascarpone
    frosting 114

  quick double chocolate sheet cake
    102

  raspberry and white chocolate
    muffins 119

  St. Clement's drizzle cake 108

carrots 14

beet and carrot purée 155

  spicy carrot, tomato, chorizo, and
    cilantro soup 43

  velvety butternut squash soup 48

cauliflower 14

  cauliflower and broccoli cheese
    with ham and tomatoes 166

cheese 12, 13

  bacon, cheddar, and sunflower
    squares 113

  cauliflower and broccoli cheese
    with ham and tomatoes 166

  cheesy spinach and pea pasta 162

  chicken, Taleggio, and spinach
    pancakes 85

  creamy zucchini, leek, and
    Parmesan soup 44

  eggplant and lentil moussaka 91

  fennel, leek, and potato gratin 84

  leek and blue cheese tarts 58

  pasta under the sea 163

chicken 12, 13

  chicken liver parfait 54

  chicken stock 27

  chicken with chorizo, bell peppers,
    and olives 84

  chicken with white wine and herbs 35

  chicken, ham, and tarragon pie 86

  chicken, Taleggio, and spinach
    crêpes 85

  coconut, chicken, and butternut
    squash curry 66

  first chicken four ways 156

  sticky chicken 167

chiles 14

  Thai green curry paste 37

chocolate

  choca-mocha loaf with mascarpone
    frosting 114

chocolate and mint vodka 137
dark chocolate pots 139
dark chocolate sauce 20
quick double chocolate sheet cake
  102
raspberry and white chocolate
  muffins 119
white chocolate sauce 20
chorizo
  chicken with chorizo, bell peppers,
    and olives 84
  spicy carrot, tomato, chorizo, and
    cilantro soup 43
Christmas turnovers 146
cilantro
  spicy carrot, tomato, chorizo, and
    cilantro soup 43
coconut, chicken, and butternut
  squash curry 66
coffee
  choca-mocha loaf with mascarpone
    frosting 114
cookies 12
  freezer cookies 104–5
crab
  crab cakes with citrus and avocado
    salad 88
  smoked fish, crab, and watercress
    tart 94
cream 12, 13
  custard sauce 30
creamy zucchini, leek, and Parmesan
  soup 44
crêpes 12, 30
  chicken, Taleggio, and spinach
    crêpes 85
cucumber 14
  gazpacho 47
curries
  aromatic lamb curry 97
  coconut, chicken, and butternut
    squash curry 66
  Thai green curry paste 37
custard sauce 30
dark chocolate pots 139
dark chocolate sauce 20

easy mince pies 116
eggplant 14
  eggplant and lentil moussaka 91
eggs 12, 13
  custard sauce 30
  fish pot pies 69
entertaining 6, 8
fennel 15
  fennel, leek, and potato gratin 84
  pork belly with cracklings, fennel,
    and shallots 76
finnan haddie chowder 51
first chicken four ways 156
first fish four ways 158–9
fish 12
  finnan haddie chowder 51
  first fish four ways 158–9
  fish pot pies 69
  fish pie with hidden vegetables 169
  pasta under the sea 163
  smoked fish, crab, and watercress
    tart 94
  smoked trout pâté 54
  zucchini and corn cakes with
    smoked salmon 56
flageolet beans
  pork and flageolet bean stew 75
flavored vodkas 137
freezer cookies 104–5
freezing 8–9, 65
  boxes and bags 10
  labeling 10
  storage times 12
  thawing 11
fruit 6, 14–15
  fruit cage puddings 136
  fruit juice 13
  storage times 12
USDA advice 11
game terrine with pink peppercorns 55
garlic bread 38
gazpacho 47
golden raisins
  Christmas turnovers 146
  golden raisin scones 112
granola bars, healthier 106

ground beef 12
  ground beef for all occasions 34
  mini hamburgers with honey glaze
    164
ham 12
  cauliflower and broccoli cheese
    with ham and tomatoes 166
  chicken, ham, and tarragon pie 86
hard cider
  pork chops with mustard, apples,
    and cider 72
herbs 12, 13
  chicken with white wine and herbs 35
honey
  honey and almond cookies 105
  mini hamburgers with honey glaze
    164
honeycomb ice cream 122
ice cream
  black and red ice cream 128
  black and red terrine 130
  no-churn vanilla ice cream 124
  nutty honeycomb ice cream 122
  rhubarb crunch ice cream 127
  strawberry and meringue ice cream
    125
ice pops 140
lamb 12
  aromatic lamb curry 97
  lamb and prune tagine 83
  slow-roast shoulder of lamb 92
  smart shepherd's pie 93
  spicy lamb kabobs 62
lasagna 13
  beef and spinach lasagna 98
late summer frangipane tart 144
leeks 15
  creamy zucchini, leek, and
    Parmesan soup 44
  fennel, leek, and potato gratin 84
  leek and blue cheese tarts 58
leftovers 6, 8, 13
lemons 13
  St. Clement's drizzle cake 108
lentils
  eggplant and lentil moussaka 91

chocolate and mint vodka 137
dark chocolate pots 139
dark chocolate sauce 20
quick double chocolate sheet cake 102
raspberry and white chocolate muffins 119
white chocolate sauce 20
chorizo
chicken with chorizo, bell peppers, and olives 84
spicy carrot, tomato, chorizo, and cilantro soup 43
Christmas turnovers 146
cilantro
spicy carrot, tomato, chorizo, and cilantro soup 43
coconut, chicken, and butternut squash curry 66
coffee
choca-mocha loaf with mascarpone frosting 114
cookies 12
freezer cookies 104–5
crab
crab cakes with citrus and avocado salad 88
smoked fish, crab, and watercress tart 94
cream 12, 13
custard sauce 30
creamy zucchini, leek, and Parmesan soup 44
crêpes 12, 30
chicken, Taleggio, and spinach crêpes 85
cucumber 14
gazpacho 47
curries
aromatic lamb curry 97
coconut, chicken, and butternut squash curry 66
Thai green curry paste 37
custard sauce 30
dark chocolate pots 139
dark chocolate sauce 20

easy mince pies 116
eggplant 14
eggplant and lentil moussaka 91
eggs 12, 13
custard sauce 30
fish pot pies 69
entertaining 6, 8
fennel 15
fennel, leek, and potato gratin 84
pork belly with cracklings, fennel, and shallots 76
finnan haddie chowder 51
first chicken four ways 156
first fish four ways 158–9
fish 12
finnan haddie chowder 51
first fish four ways 158–9
fish pot pies 69
fish pie with hidden vegetables 169
pasta under the sea 163
smoked fish, crab, and watercress tart 94
smoked trout pâté 54
zucchini and corn cakes with smoked salmon 56
flageolet beans
pork and flageolet bean stew 75
flavored vodkas 137
freezer cookies 104–5
freezing 8–9, 65
boxes and bags 10
labeling 10
storage times 12
thawing 11
fruit 6, 14–15
fruit cage puddings 136
fruit juice 13
storage times 12
USDA advice 11
game terrine with pink peppercorns 55
garlic bread 38
gazpacho 47
golden raisins
Christmas turnovers 146
golden raisin scones 112
granola bars, healthier 106

ground beef 12
ground beef for all occasions 34
mini hamburgers with honey glaze 164
ham 12
cauliflower and broccoli cheese with ham and tomatoes 166
chicken, ham, and tarragon pie 86
hard cider
pork chops with mustard, apples, and cider 72
herbs 12, 13
chicken with white wine and herbs 35
honey
honey and almond cookies 105
mini hamburgers with honey glaze 164
honeycomb ice cream 122
ice cream
black and red ice cream 128
black and red terrine 130
no-churn vanilla ice cream 124
nutty honeycomb ice cream 122
rhubarb crunch ice cream 127
strawberry and meringue ice cream 125
ice pops 140
lamb 12
aromatic lamb curry 97
lamb and prune tagine 83
slow-roast shoulder of lamb 92
smart shepherd's pie 93
spicy lamb kabobs 62
lasagna 13
beef and spinach lasagna 98
late summer frangipane tart 144
leeks 15
creamy zucchini, leek, and Parmesan soup 44
fennel, leek, and potato gratin 84
leek and blue cheese tarts 58
leftovers 6, 8, 13
lemons 13
St. Clement's drizzle cake 108
lentils
eggplant and lentil moussaka 91

sausage baked with Puy lentils 74
limes 13
    mojito sherbet 133
Madeira sauce 24
mango
    pear and mango purée 153
mascarpone frosting
    choca-mocha loaf with mascarpone
      frosting 114
meringues 12
    black and red terrine 130
    strawberry and meringue ice cream
      125
    individual meringues 135
mince pies, easy 116
mint
    chocolate and mint vodka 137
mojito sherbet 133
moussaka, eggplant, and lentil 91
muffins
    raspberry and white chocolate
      muffins 119
mushrooms
    fish pot pies 69
    ox cheeks with red wine and
      mushrooms 99
    shrimp and noodle broth 71
mustard
    pork chops with mustard, apples,
      and cider 72
    sausage rolls with mustard and
      poppy seed 52
no-churn vanilla ice cream 124
noodles
    shrimp and noodle broth 71
nuts
    blueberry, almond, and orange
      cupcakes 111
    nutty honeycomb ice cream 122
    syrup, orange, and walnut tart 142
oats
    healthier granola bars 106
    oat crumble 147
olives

chicken with chorizo, bell peppers,
    and olives 84
onions
    Portuguese seafood stew 68
    sausage baked with Puy lentils 74
    velvety butternut squash soup 48
oranges 12, 13
    blueberry, almond, and orange
      cupcakes 111
    crab cakes with citrus and avocado
      salad 88
    St. Clement's drizzle cake 108
    syrup, orange, and walnut tart 142
ox cheeks with red wine and
    mushrooms 99
pasta
    beef and spinach lasagna 98
    cheesy spinach and pea pasta 162
    pasta under the sea 163
pavlovas 12
    pavlova with pomegranates and
      raspberries 134–5
pears 15
    apple and pear purée 153
    Christmas turnovers 146
    pear and mango purée 153
peas 15
    asparagus and pea risotto 74
    cheesy spinach and pea pasta 162
    watercress and pea soup 46
peppers 15
    chicken with chorizo, bell peppers,
      and olives 84
    Portuguese seafood stew 68
    bell pepper and sweet potato purée
      154
    sausage baked with Puy lentils 74
pie dough 12, 13
    pie dough 28
    sweet pie dough 28
pizza 160
pomegranates
    pavlova with pomegranates and
      raspberries 134–5

pomegranate vodka 137
    spicy lamb kabobs 62
poppy seed
    sausage rolls with mustard and
      poppy seed 52
pork 12
    game terrine with pink peppercorns
      55
    pork and flageolet bean stew 75
    pork belly with cracklings, fennel,
      and shallots 76
    pork chops with mustard, apples,
      and cider 72
Portuguese seafood stew 68
potatoes 13, 15
    fennel, leek, and potato gratin 84
    smart shepherd's pie 93
    two potato mash 159
prunes
    game terrine with pink peppercorns
      55
    lamb and prune tagine 83
purées 12, 152
    apple and blackberry purée 154
    apple and pear purée 153
    beet and carrot purée 155
    pear and mango purée 153
    bell pepper and sweet potato purée
      154
quiches 12
quick double chocolate sheet cake 102
rabbit
    game terrine with pink peppercorns
      55
raspberries 15
    fruit cage puddings 136
    late summer frangipane tart 144
    pavlova with pomegranates and
      raspberries 134–5
    raspberry and apple crumble 148
    raspberry and white chocolate
      muffins 119
bell pepper and sweet potato purée
    154

acknowledgments

I'm so incredibly grateful to all my family and friends who have been kind enough to test recipes from the book to make sure they are in tip-top shape:

Katherine Coltart, Simon and Ness Baker, Harry Cox, Mel Clegg, Ems Bray, Mrs Edgecombe, Gemma Pearce, Judy Snell, Andrea Eles, Isabel Sandison, Katie James, Marcia Ritchie, Clare Evelyn, Tania MacCallum, Lesley Sandison, Soph Martin, Jane Brooke, Els Rooth, Anna Greenhalgh, Alex Nolon, Claire Davies, Anna Broome, Jane Wiggs, Lucy Urquhart, Rebecca Bone, Ali Palmer, Katherine McNamara, Katie Callard, Debbie Sandison, and Gill Head. You are all wonderful!

Yet again, extra special thanks go to my brother, mother, and mother-in-law, all of whom have been happy to ponder book ideas over the phone, share their recipes, and drop everything to help with both cooking and child minding—big, big thanks to you!

Thanks also to Georgie Sangiorgio and Claire Davies, who worked their way through all the recipes, checking the copy made sense, giving feedback, and generally getting me organized!

Catharine, Estella, Jenny, Victoria, Emma, and the rest of the team at Kyle Cathie are all supreme champions as far as I'm concerned. They have put up with many a weird question and whim without the slightest flicker of annoyance throughout the entire process of making this book, as with my previous one!

Kyle, I am hugely grateful to you for giving me this incredible opportunity—I hope I do you proud.

Last, but not least, thanks to A, W, and J, who have been encouraging, patient, supportive, and in general just all-round superstars. Thanks for munching your way through the entire book, even when at early stages of testing! All I will say is, at least it's a bit more varied than jam!